You need this book if y

- Wanting to change career
- Looking for a new job
- Uncertain how to navigate the digitised job market
- Someone who hates interviews and selling yourself
- Worried you might be made redundant
- Thinking of resigning
- Trying to find your transferable skills to change sectors or job role
- Facing a promotion panel
- Returning to work after a break
- Bored with CV writing and LinkedIn
- Wondering what to do next
- Working parent or carer
- A graduate
- A new interim or contractor
- An older professional
- A freelancer or a self-employed consultant
- Trying to negotiate a fair rate for your work
- Lacking confidence
- A disabled worker or job-seeker
- Feeling like an impostor
- Wondering what your next move is
- Looking for post-retirement or portfolio projects
- Lacking a network or think you are rubbish at networking
- Struggling to get recruiters to return your calls?
- Nervous of negotiating a pay rise
- Frightened of fitting in to selective, middle-class organisations
- Feeling stuck or frustrated at work
- Concerned you need to sharpen your career management skills
- Certain you can do better in your career but don't know how.

What you'll get from this book...

- Everything you need to fire up your career; from working out your skillset; negotiating offers, maintaining a long-term career strategy, from graduation to retirement
- An alternative to bragging and boasting
- A cliché free interview style for job searches and promotion boards, which makes you the obvious, no brainer candidate
- A process to halve the time it takes to find better work: permanent; freelance; contract; part-time; or portfolio
- Techniques for working out what you are best at; the type of work most meaningful for you; and your transferable skills
- Special sections for graduates, women, working parents, disabled candidates, mature workers and returners
- A CV that gets you in front of people and through the filters
- A personal statement, which you are proud of
- Understanding the black arts of the recruitment industry, so your calls are returned
- A LinkedIn profile that makes you visible and found
- Proven tactics for passing interviews and internal promotion panels using great case studies
- Demystified competency based interviews
- Answers for questions they shouldn't ask you but want to
- Networking skills, which help you get round the 'jobs for the boys' culture
- Ways to make direct approaches
- Help, if you are starting off as a freelancer or in self-employment
- Tricks to work out your transferable skills and how to change careers

- Common sense reasons why you are more successful than you think
- A career strategy to avoid future derailment and build on your success
- Loss of fear of selling yourself

I know this works

For 15 years I owned a business that recruited other recruiters, yes, you read that right. That's got to be the sharpest end of the recruitment business, placing recruitment consultants in other recruitment consultancies. My network is with those recruiters and headhunters and I understand how recruiter's minds and their algorithms work. They are constantly telling me how fed up they are hearing the same old trite nonsense at interview and reading it in CVs.

When I sold up, I gained a masters degree in organisational psychology with a career management specialism and qualified as an executive coach, using mostly cognitive behavioural techniques. Now, I coach hundreds of clients each year to make smarter moves, either in their own organisation or on the job market. I work with individuals and I run group career development workshops and I'm proud to say that people recommend their colleagues and friends to me to be 'Zenafied.' I have now helped thousands of people to get hired, promoted or make sense of their careers and they all have used my recommended techniques.

Ines

wishing you success
& happiness,

Zena

Published by
Filament Publishing Ltd
16 Croydon Road, Beddington, Croydon,
Surrey, CR0 4PA, United Kingdom.
Telephone +44 (0)20 8688 2598
www.filamentpublishing.com

© 2017 Zena Everett

The right of Zena Everett to be recognised as the author of this work
has been asserted by her in accordance with the
Designs and Copyright Act 1988.

ISBN 978-1-911425-70-0

Printed by IngramSpark.

MIND
FLIP

ZENA EVERETT

The new manual for career shifters and job seekers

What other people are saying about this book

'It is refreshing to see a career book that unpicks the bias in organisations - and in our own heads - that stop us from fulfilling our dreams. Whether you're facing the glass ceiling or the class ceiling, this book helps you understand how to break through it, and get on.'
Mary Creagh MP

'If you take your career seriously, this is the only book you need to read. Zena Everett has more knowledge, experience and insight as to how recruiters work and corporates hire than anyone I know.'
Ann Swain, CEO, Association of Professional Staffing Companies

'Zena Everett is a fresh and original voice in the careers field.'
John Lees, author of *How to Get a Job You Love*

'Zena's book stands out from the field and is not simply another self-help book. Great advice here on how to request flexible working, manage the topic of children at interviews (the baby elephant in the room) and get what you want. Work isn't about hours or location any more; it's about achieving objectives. Mind Flip will make you stronger and help you achieve your personal career goals.'
Gill Stewart, Managing Director, Capability Jane

'My career path was obscure after giving up my career to be a full time mother. With Zena's guidance to restore my confidence and help me to find clarity, I fulfilled my deep-rooted ambition to become a successful freelance writer. I published my first book and was delighted with the reviews I received and am now writing my second. The information in Mind Flip is invaluable.'
Dr Christine L Corton: Author of *London Fog: The Biography*: voted an Evening Standard Best Book and a Telegraph Christmas Best Book 2015

'Zena really challenges the status quo in Mind Flip. If you are fed up in your job, want a change or new direction; you need to take personal responsibility to do something about it. This book can help you. Zena talks through how to make shifts and developments to your career and think about what you can deliver to your boss to create a win-win outcome. She brings unique and refreshing insights, having worked at the sharp end of headhunting before studying for a Masters in Career Management and Counseling to embark on her own career change.'
James Bennet MBE, Director, Ernst & Young LLP

'Finally, a careers book that realises that people 50+ are still ambitious. As Zena says, just because we are no longer reproductive, doesn't mean we aren't productive! I love this book and so do my sons, my husband and my Mum.'
Ann Stephens, Co-Founder www.hotflush.info

'With a job for life no longer attainable, nor desirable and the world of work evolving at speed, everyone will need to prepare themselves for a career of shifts, changes and personal reinventions. This means rethinking the way you look at yourself. Zena Everett is the perfect guide for this journey of discovery and change and her book Mind Flip is the manual you'll need with you all the way.'
Mervyn Dinnen, Talent and HR Analyst, Speaker, Blogger, Author 'Exceptional Talent' www.exceptionaltalent.io

'I love the concept of being Marmite and not Vanilla; being brave enough to drill down into your skills and what you uniquely do. This book is an enormous confidence boost.'
Dr Emily Pringle, Head of Learning Practice and Research, Tate

'Mind Flip is a rich source of insight and experience, delivered with punch and humour: a valuable investment of your time.'
Lara Morgan, sold her majority share in Pacific Direct for £20m and is now a Venture Capitalist and founder of www.companyshortcuts.com

'Comprehensive, smart and accessible - an excellent guide to successful career management.'
Alan Stewart, Partner, Blackwood Group (Executive Search)

'Post 50 can be a time when people become more ambitious, not less and will continue to contribute their expertise, wisdom and emotional intelligence to the workplace. It is really important to help those of all ages find the tools they need to find their niche and manage their career.'
Baroness Ros Altmann, CBE

'Mind Flip reflects the modern, blended workplace; Millennials working with Generation Z and freelancers working side by side with permanent employees. Wherever you fit, you need to stand out in a highly competitive talent pool and Zena's techniques will give you the tools and inspiration you need.'
Dan Torjussen-Proctor, Chief Operating Officer, Parker Fitzgerald

'I've known Zena for 20 years and respect her knowledge and views enormously. I'm delighted she has taken the time to put much of her wisdom into this book. At one level it's a deeply practical guide to help you get what you want from your career, but what really sets it apart is the way Zena challenges our often flawed thinking in this space and offers a wonderfully powerful alternative. And for me it's this alternative that's so inspiring, not just for your career but more fundamentally in terms of how you might choose to live your life.'
Simon La Fosse, CEO, La Fosse Associates (Top 20 Sunday Times Best 100 Companies to Work For 2013, 2014, 2015, 2016, 2017 and Top 100 Fastest Growing Company in the UK. The Sunday Times Virgin Fast Track 2011, 2013, 2014)

'Zena's advice is brilliant. It's sensible as well as entertaining and it's based on years of real-life experience in recruitment. Buy this book!'
Sir Richard John Evans, President of Wolfson College, Cambridge and Provost of Gresham College.

'Mind Flip is like having Zena in your pocket, guaranteed to get you fired up and your career racing forward.'
Wayne Reynolds, Headhunter and CEO Birchwood Knight

About Zena Everett

Zena is an international executive coach, with a rare cocktail of entrepreneurial, headhunting, organisational psychology and coaching experience. She started and ran her own recruitment business and became fascinated with why some of her candidates were more motivated, confident and successful than others. To figure that out, she sold her business, completed a Masters in Career Management and Counselling and undertook further post-graduate coaching training. She now helps ambitious people to achieve career goals they didn't know they had, or were capable of until they worked with her.

Brought up in Ireland, Zena coaches people from many different cultures and backgrounds, from actors to actuaries and mum returners to MBAs, coaching on the Executive MBA programme at Oxford University's Saïd Business School.

Zena has a wealth of experience and a respected reputation amongst recruiters and headhunters, who send candidates to her to be 'Zenafied.'

Her recruitment business recruited other recruiters – so not only was she a recruiter - she was a recruiter's recruiter. This gave her unique inside knowledge of how recruitment consultants evaluate CVs and why some candidates make it through filtering processes and others don't. She comes from the sharpest end of the recruitment business and demystifies the black arts of this industry. Her dissertation provided unique insights into how recruiters, HR professional and employers evaluate the personal statements on CVs and she draws on this in her first book, *Mind Flip*.

Zena is a regular media contributor on career and workplace issues (BBC London: Careers Agony Aunt with Jeni Barnett; LBC; BBC 5 Live; BBC Berkshire; Sky News; Radio 4 Today Programme; BBC One Breakfast; The Guardian; The Financial Times; High50; Cosmopolitan; and Vice). She is passionate about raising the confidence and ambition of people at work and is a popular, inspirational speaker at conferences and events.

She is a non-executive director and trustee of Quo Vadis Trust, a social housing charity that supports people with mental ill health. Zena lives in London and is writing books.

To view details of her events and to sign up to her mailing list please visit: **www.zenaeverett.com**

To watch a two minute animation of the Mind Flip process visit Zena's YouTube channel or cut and past this into your browser: **https://youtu.be/VDpuj8IE1Ns**

For Alannah, Gabriel, Sam and Rose

Acknowledgements

Mind Flip was inspired by all the people I have worked with, interviewed, placed in jobs, not placed in jobs, worked for, been hired by, coached, trained and presented for. As they say where I come from, thanks a million.

Getting a first book published isn't easy and I am particularly grateful to the people who have helped me to find my voice and make it happen. These are: Jane Graham Maw, Peter Godden, David Glassman, Chris Day, Jane Malin and particularly, my editor, Wendy Yorke. Who knew there were things called 'crutch words' or that I would use so many of them?

Huge thanks to all of you.

Foreword by DeeDee Doke

'Wouldn't it be great if recruitment worked something like this: an organisation issues a public announcement inviting anyone interested in working there to come in; tell the recruiters about themselves and what they'd like to do; and get placed in such a role immediately; or at the minimum, be placed in a talent pool to await an opening in that field? In this scenario, the organisation is able to flex salaries up or down, depending on its needs at the moment and on an individual's aptitudes and experiences.

I like that idea. It's simplistic to the max, and gets rid of most of the trappings of the pseudo-science that recruitment is often made out to be. Perhaps it's too simple. Don't get me wrong - I believe in recruitment as a practice - which when done well is more alchemy than science. But lately I've been thinking more that it's an unduly painful process for everyone involved.

A job is, arguably, a person's greatest asset. On a practical level, it generates the resources that pay for life's basic necessities, including shelter, food and clothing etc. Less tangibly, a job offers purpose, skills development, status and even enjoyment.

But what is a career? A collection of jobs and experiences? A flesh-and-blood CV? Years ago, a career might best have been thought of as the pursuit of one's life work through a series of jobs with one employer. Today, a career is more dynamic, fluid and mysterious because there are fewer 'sure things' in the world of work.

It's almost a cliché to say that we live in a time of unprecedented technological change, a noisy revolution, which has meant that employers' skills requirements change regularly and multi-fold. New types of jobs abound. Look at most workplaces and see teams and divisions that did not exist in their current form until very recently and are continuing to 'morph' into still something else entirely.

The workplace is also undergoing incredible cultural change: consider the focus of major employers on diversifying their workforces and reaching out to people of every kind. The capability of working from different locations including one's home, the life demands that require a more flexible approach to working hours, the creation of physical workplaces that help or encourage people to feel and do their best at work. The engagement of multi-generational workforces, these are just a few of the factors contributing to this revolution.

Then there's another simple little contribution that comes down to the individual, heightened by the technological changes and the reliance on connection and instant information; the constant distractions from those little 'alert' notifications. We have shorter attention spans and we make more job changes more quickly than we used to.

Of course, some moves are prompted by a quest for better money and perks - probably not the best drivers for ultimate happiness - with the aim of securing more and more and more material wealth and status.

A more profound way of looking at a career is putting it in the context of personal identity and allowing it to raise a multitude of questions as if you were sitting outside yourself as an objective interviewer. Who am I as a human being at this time in my life? How does my work at this moment reflect my skills and interests, my cultural and geographical preferences for a workplace, my outside life, my personal needs and my aspirations? What kind of experience am I having in my work? What are the standout propositions of this job for me? What do I want to be good at? What talents do I have – as opposed to skills – which I don't get to use in this job? How am I changing as a person? What role does this particular 'stop', or job, play on my long-term path? What meaning does it have? Do I want a 'step ladder' approach to my career? What do I want to do and where do I want to go next? What do I want to learn? Is there an ultimate destination or do I want to collect interesting and enjoyable experiences? Who am I?

In our contemporary multi-track existences, many of us also run parallel careers. Unpaid or volunteer work can become nearly full-time jobs and in those roles, we ask ourselves the same searching questions. However, we often answer those questions more honestly and open-heartedly because we are giving and not being paid for, our time. What if we applied this same internal honesty and open-heartedness to the questions we ask about our paid work?

At the same time, those questions you're asking yourself are generally of less interest to a paying employer – unless you and your skills are in the enviable position of being headhunted – than they are to you.

From my observer's position, sitting both inside the recruitment industry and profession and slightly outside it, I see a fragmented picture of contemporary recruiting. New technology tools and techniques are intended to find the 'right' or the 'best' person for a job and yet old-fashioned visions of who or what the 'right/best' person is, or even what the job should be in the organisation's future state of play. This condition also sees organisations still stunningly poor at dealing with applicants who are not selected for interview or, after interview, not selected.

I see organisations that cannot properly identify the aptitudes, attitudes and skills that are needed to progress the 'business' – whether for profit, not-for-profit, charity, or public sector and recruiting individuals who will simply continue what has been. And there is still too much 'comfort zone' recruitment, promotion and sadly, retention.

Part of the blame for the continuation of these old-fashioned problems in a new-fangled world is the expectation that technology alone solves any issue.

An ever bigger part I believe, is the overwhelming nature of the business world we live in now, with which most organisations have not gotten to grips. To say it is a Herculean job for anyone in work, from the least experienced to those at the top is an understatement. From political upheaval to the omnipresent complexities of social media, technology, increasing regulatory requirements and evolving work styles, the avalanche of change is relentless. Creating and executing Plan A's take up so much time, no one has enough capacity to develop Plan B or Plan C thinking.

Where does that leave the job seeker and the career strategist? This is a heady, exhilarating time to be in the world of work. What choices we have to shape our individual futures! The ability to see and savour blue sky beyond the tangle of challenge is essential. But it's equally crucial in this volatile, uncertain, complex and ambiguous world to be able to explore and act on your career ambitions with dead-eyed precision and self-knowledge.

In the back catalogue of ancient music videos, an irreverent classic by an American band that performed in drag, Twisted Sister, comes to mind when I think about careers and life generally. Before the band breaks into the song "We're Not Going to Take It" the father of the video's young hero bawls at his son "What do you want to DO with your life?" The son's answer: "I want to ROCK!"

Rock on and be happy, whatever your definition of that is!'

DeeDee Doke
Editor, Recruiter magazine/recruiter.co.uk

Contents

'Yerra, what about it, sure wasn't I at least the author of my own tale? And if you can say that as you depart this world, you can say a lot.'

Lily, in Donal Ryan's *The Spinning Heart*

INTRODUCTION

Think in the other direction

There is a simple, yet profound shift you can make that to help find better work, change careers and ultimately find fulfilment in what you do. It is simply to stop thinking about yourself. Instead shift your focus from your circumstances to the circumstances of those around you. Change your narrative to look in the other direction, not on you, but on the solution you offer to other people. The value you uniquely provide.

Let me explain. Pursuing success for success's sake – the extrinsic or intrinsic rewards you get from doing well – will not on their own give your career real meaning. Research has found only a modest correlation between income and happiness. If you are at the top of the ladder but not feeling as satisfied as you thought you should be by now, you may have lost a sense of connection with your work.

Fifty years of study into happiness have taught us that social relationships are crucial components of wellbeing. Maintaining people connection is a vital part of career happiness too.

Reconnect. Think about the problems you solved for other people through your career and flip your attention on successfully doing just that. Fulfilment will inevitably follow.

A reassuring result of applying this Mind Flip is that you can stop the painful, even cheesy process of selling yourself at promotion panels or interviews. Most of us hate these. Employers ultimately care about their problems and how you can fix them.

Talk about how you give a great experience to their customers, or help their pupils pass their exams, or raise the finest vegetables to sell, or create the most environmentally friendly product, or fix a fault, or streamline a process or even solve a problem they haven't spotted they are going to come up against? Whatever the context, it usually boils down to how they can make more money, or get more funding, if you are on their payroll.

Figure out what makes an employer wake up in the middle of the night worrying and explain how you can fix their pain. That is the value you bring. Then show evidence of it, by giving examples of how you have done something similar in the past, using the same skillset. It's much easier to talk about what we can do for other people than to talk about ourselves.

Life is a circle - what goes around - comes around eventually. Since so many people are out to only help themselves, when you genuinely seek to help other people succeed in getting what they need, they will notice you. These people will in turn fight to help you succeed in getting everything you need too. *Mind Flip* will show you how to flip your mind and look in the other direction, out, not in. This is the route map for career happiness, wherever you are in your career.

This book is in four parts. The first part *Figure it out* will help you figure out the unique value you provide. Why should someone hire you, or use your services? The second part *Crack on* gives you the practical tools and techniques to launch your job search, in the quickest and most straightforward way, to find a new job, gain promotion or find the freelance work you want. The third section *Just for you* is if you need extra help to get you to where you want to be. The final part *Fulfill it* helps you to keep going, to maintain your network, keep raising the bar on your aspirations and achieve the ambitions you previously thought were impossible; or maybe you didn't know you had. What would you do next if you knew you could not fail?

Let's do it.

Mind Flipping; to flip your focus away from yourself and instead look outwards - on to the value you add and the problems you, uniquely, can solve for other people.

PART
1

FIGURE IT OUT

In this chapter I am going to show you that you don't need to tell people how fabulous you are anymore. In future, you are going to show, through the facts on your CV and case studies in your interviews, exactly what you have done in the past for previous employers. This is the best indicator of how valuable you are and what you can do in the future, for other people and specifically for the company you want to work for i.e. the interview panel. They will figure out your fabulousness for themselves.

CHAPTER 1

Flip your mind

Interviewer: *'Tell me about yourself...'*

Interviewee: *'Well, er, basically I am a natural leader, a really hard worker and a perfect fit for this job.'*

Ever said anything like that? I have listened to answers like this more times than I can bear to think about. As an ex-recruiter and executive coach I have helped thousands of people change jobs and make career changes. Most of us are naturally humble, but the groupthink is that you have to show off to find work. I might not like reading this but I know that people hate saying this even more. Meanwhile all interviewers want is a straight talking explanation of why you are better and different from the other candidates together with firm evidence to back it up. I help my clients to stop boasting and flip around how they find better work. They either avoid interview processes altogether (by going through the back door), or stick to objective facts, which they can sell confidently. In fact to the point where they feel so proud of what they do they actually enjoy interviews and changing roles. They leave the ego at the door and they talk about what they do rather than themselves.

I had been thinking about writing this book for many years and the catalyst for starting was when I was running a workshop for people at risk of redundancy. One of the participants showed me a CV, including the personal statement as shown below, which had been cobbled together from advice found on a website.

'Dynamic individual with a successful track record of goal achievement and delivery in competitive environments. Works well as an individual or in a team, results-driven and an analytical problem solver. Now seeking a fresh challenge where I can develop my career to the next level.'

They hated it too! Now, I don't know about you, but I have never been in a business where someone said, 'let's get a dynamic individual who can work well as an individual or in a team for this job'. We talk about what they want them to do and the experience they need, not character traits. But why do so many smart people fall into the trap of thinking they have to use these clichés to get a job these days? And then they wonder why they never get job offers? Somehow, when it comes to attending interviews and writing CVs - in fact the whole job search process - common sense is completely suspended. It drives me crazy. I couldn't find a readable book, which addressed the problem of this emphasised hyperbole head on, sorted out all other career misconceptions and made people feel happier and confident. So I decided to write my own.

You are not alone in hating both interviews and putting yourself out there.

I produced a webinar on transferable skills for a recruitment consultancy called Capability Jane. Below are several of the questions I was asked, which I think are pretty common from most people I work with. No one likes to blow their own trumpet.

- How do I sell my skill set and boost my confidence?
- I am in a job rut and can't sell myself.
- How do I improve my CV, which is not proving successful, without sounding obnoxious?
- I need a new job urgently, but never get any job offers because someone else had more relevant experience than me. What am I doing wrong?
- I am desperately seeking a change of direction/new career and don't know how to convince someone I am the right candidate.
- I hate talking about myself at interviews and always do badly at them.

Yet, despite the fact that most of us hate selling ourselves, why do we feel under pressure to brag when looking for another job? Or humble brag, you know the self-deprecating alternative: *'My weakness? Oh that's my perfectionism, the desire to do a 100% job for you, which means I can find myself staying late in the office trying to do a brilliant job'.* I'm sorry but it is just nauseating to sell yourself like this, people can see through it a mile off!

It's this style of selling, which has become the problem. It rarely works and misses the whole point of why you are there. The person you are meeting wants to know what you can do for them. On the one side there's you and your experience. On the other is the employer and their self-interest. You have to join the dots and provide evidence that you can solve their problems. That's all it takes to motivate them to hire you.

Stop selling yourself.
Sell what you do for other people.

You are not there to tell them about you, your career history and where you are currently. You are there to explain, simply, how you can fix their pain. The most important element is the end result. The value you bring. How can a potential employer make more money or save money if you are on their payroll? Successful careers are built by focusing on this value. Explaining it in an objective, evidence based way because you are no longer spewing out lists of personal characteristics. You are selling facts. Not bull.

The fact of the matter is ...it's all about facts from now on.

Step into their shoes.

The truth is, recruiters and employers don't actually care about you. What they care about is how they are going to become better when you work for them. What problems can you solve for them and what outcomes will you get for them? They might only glance at your CV for a few seconds. You need to make them select you, before they move on to the next applicant. The way to do this is to step out of your shoes and wear theirs. What keeps them awake at night? Think of the problems you solve and what you do for other people better than everyone else. Understand their problem and present yourself as the solution with solid data, not hollow boasts and lists of action words. Just facts.

I am going to teach you how to switch your interview technique, your CV writing and your LinkedIn profile - in fact your whole job search and career strategy - so it's not about you. It is all about the problems you solve. I will make you stand out as the obvious candidate and help you change how you approach your career forever.

You might think this is a cool, contemporary approach to getting a job and indeed it is. However, it was Aristotle who observed 2500 years ago that; 'Where the needs of the world and your talents cross, there lies your vocation.' In this, as in so much, the ancients got it spot on. It's the basic principle of selling. You find

1

out what the person's problem is and sell them a solution. In this case, that's you. We have lost sight of this wisdom and common sense, in a cloud of adverbs.

I am in that middle-aged stage where my patience is low and my tolerance for bragging is even lower. I hate CVs full of nonsense and no facts. I know that people in recruitment hate them even more because they get hundreds of them in their inboxes every week. Finding good candidates is getting increasingly harder. The Internet is crammed with confusing advice of all qualities on how to write CVs and apply for jobs. The digital world opens up so many career opportunities while obfuscating the quickest paths to finding better work

When I started out, people would print off a load of CVs and drop them off by hand. It worked because they showed energy and commitment. Now job seekers fire off CVs, or worse, they press the automatic application button on job boards and sit and wait for a magic hand, like the one on the National Lottery ads, to pluck them out of the swamp of other job seekers. Actually, not enough people pick up the phone these days and make things happen and I want to put that right. I know it's difficult to get through the firewall around employers these days but in this book I am going to teach you several methods to do it. Best of all, these methods work for everyone, especially people who hate any kind of sales and those of us from outside the traditional talent pool, who need to break into majority networks from the outside. You don't have to be one of the boys.

If you are still wondering how you answer the; *'Tell me about yourself?'* question. The answer is - in a way that connects what you have done in the past - straight into the demands of their role, as the example demonstrates below.

'Well, as you can see, I've been managing complex housing renovation schemes for the last six year, up to £40 million budgets across Northern England and Scotland. I love what I do and have been lucky enough to win awards for our last two projects. The area I enjoy most is building sustainable housing and I am interested in this role because this is the focus of your organisation and I want to talk about how my experience can contribute to this.'

This is the alternative to the meaningless bragging and boasting, which people are brainwashed into coming up with at interview. Plenty more information about interview techniques later on in Chapter 7: *The Interview Minefield*.

Warning
If you really aspire to interview like a candidate on *The Apprentice* then perhaps this book is not for you. Thanks anyway, we'll be in touch. If on the other hand, all that bull is simply to cover up your vulnerabilities, then let's work out how valuable you really are and help you sell yourself more convincingly.

1

In this chapter we will look at a case study to demonstrate the Mind Flip Process. We will discover Nick's Story and how his Mind Flip enabled him to find a new role in a different sector. He learnt that was not about him, but about what he can do for other people. Then you will do your deepest thinking: figure out your own career goal, what you can do for other people and how to go about your search process, using Zena's Smart Job Search Plan.

CHAPTER 2

It's not about you; Zena's Smart Job Search Plan

Nick's Success Story

Nick had been in the music industry for most of his career - apart from a brief spell as a butcher's apprentice straight after university - when he knew he didn't want to work at a dull office job and he was experimenting with alternatives. Now in his mid 40s, he had worked his way up to become the marketing director of a record label most of us would recognise. Well, we would if we still bought records of course and that is the problem. People want access to music now rather than owning it and Nick was keeping up with a digital revolution that had changed the landscape of his industry beyond all recognition, from physical retail to global subscription services. His employer, like the other major labels was eventually merged into another giant and Nick knew he couldn't avoid the wave of redundancies that would inevitably follow. The call came and there was a gruesomely prolonged process while HR pretended that termination wasn't a slam-dunk. Three weeks, later, Nick held his leaving do in the pub round the corner.

No matter how confident and resilient we are, leaving work in these circumstances is never easy. We feel rudderless. Our personal identity is heavily tied up with the work we do. Some of us do well at work because we are control freak perfectionists and having uncertain futures hits us particularly hard. Even if we have a nice financial cushion to take away money anxieties, it seems to bring out all those critical inner voices: *'I've failed, it's all my fault, I always knew I'd get found out as a fraud. I've given them everything and it's thrown back in my face. How can they do this to me?'*

This was the first time Nick had encountered any substantial set back – he'd had a glamorous career - travelling round the world with his musical heroes in the early years and his wife and family had enjoyed the spoils of his career. He'd never experienced any kind of derailment before and he took it as a personal failure. He didn't know how to cope. The nice outplacement chap's advice that he could sign on for contribution based job seekers allowance didn't give him much comfort. What do you say when someone says, *'What do you do?'* at a dinner party.

This is where friends and family step in. Advice varies from; *'You need to get on Twitter mate, that's how everyone finds jobs these days'* to; *'My neighbour has been out of work for over a year now, he said he's sent hundreds of CVs but he is discriminated against because he is too old/not old enough/ over qualified/under qualified/too senior'*… you know the rest. Nick sat down and wrote his CV, copying the format of his son's, who had recently left university and had got help from the school careers advisor. He wrote three pages of everything he had done in his working life. He talked about: his visionary leadership capability; his outside-the-box-thinking; his sound business acumen; track record of delivery; enthusiasm for the next stage; focus on solutions; and so on. He uploaded the document onto LinkedIn. It was painful to write and fairly painful to read. He immediately sent it to other music companies – the few that weren't in the same group as his organisation – but they said that frankly they wanted to lose people at his level, not put more on the payroll. That industry had lost the shine for him anyway. He'd been in at the heyday and didn't want to take another job he knew wasn't sustainable for the sake of his reputation at the cricket club.

He applied for generic digital marketing and marketing jobs and even had some interviews. Now don't shoot the messenger, but the media industry isn't exactly known for its robust promotion processes and Nick hadn't had a proper interview or appraisal for twenty years. Questions such as; *'Tell me about a time when your leadership principles were compromised?'* floored him. But he blustered his way through with sample answers he'd got off the web on the train to the interview. He never got offers and hated selling himself like this.

I can go on to tell you more about Nick's story. But what you need to know is the happy ending, which illustrates the point of the book.

The music industry has led the way for creative industries in the digital world. Other industries, such as publishing and gaming followed through these digital phases and wanted to learn the lessons the music industry had gone through. Nick's reality check came when he realised his most valuable asset was this knowledge. He stopped bragging to headhunters about being; *'A strategic leader in periods of challenging growth'*, (which he didn't really feel like anyway). Instead, he worked out what he specifically knew about that other people didn't and wrote a one-pager bio that focused on this, listing the artists he had marketed and the market share they had gained and their sales performance. Then he wrote a list of everyone he had ever worked with who could be useful to him; where they were and how had they segued out of the music industry. He used his season ticket to travel into London to have lots of coffees, lunches and beers talking to people. Fortunately, he was an affable chap who people liked and wanted to talk to. His generosity with freebie concert tickets over the years probably helped too. So nurture your network before this happens to you.

There's a tired old concept called the elevator pitch. Generally people that have elevator pitches are the last people you want to be trapped in an elevator with. They sound tired and a bit desperate. Nick decided not to go down that route, despite all the helpful advice telling him to craft one. Nick simply talked normally to his contacts about what was going on in their business. He stopped pitching and started listening to what they needed. People love to talk about their problems to someone who will listen to them.

Nick thought about how he could differentiate himself and be the solution to their problems. He worked out that not only did he know about digital marketing in the music industry, in recent years he had been overseeing the marketing of indie pop and hip hop artists. He knew all about the online spending patterns of the consumers of this music, particularly urban youth aged 17 to 30 and he knew how to get them to spend more money. This was priceless information to sectors who wanted to sell more music to this lucrative demographic. Nick knew how to do it. He wasn't up against anyone else in an interview process because he created these opportunities for himself through his own expertise. He wasn't formally interviewed, he went through back doors - talking to CEOs not HR - because he had something they wanted.

Eventually he got a six month consultancy for a fast-growing urban youth clothes company who realised they didn't want to lose him to a competitor. They didn't care about how old he was. In fact they liked the maturity he bought to their leadership team. Before his contract was up they put him on the payroll with a better package than he was on before and the security of knowing that provided he continued to do a good job, he was in an industry that would continue to need him. If he chose to change jobs, he had a network and a reputation within it for particular marketing knowledge and expertise. He's now moved industries to demonstrate that he understands more than one sector.

1

Nick's Action Plan
What he did

- He worked out specifically what he knew about that other people didn't: his expertise. He knew where his skillset was valuable.
- He stopped looking for jobs and instead thought about companies who had problems he could solve.
- He presented himself as the solution to those problems, backed with data to prove he had already solved them on someone else's payroll.
- He explained the value of what he did.
- He didn't fuss about his weaknesses. He simply did what he was best at.

What he didn't do

- He didn't wait for the "right job" to be presented to him.
- He created his own opportunities so he wasn't in competition with anyone else.
- He didn't brag or boast or bluff his way through a process - he simply talked in specific terms about what he could do for them - and he didn't pretend to be someone he wasn't.
- He didn't say he was open to opportunities - he was very specific about what he did - and what he didn't.

I am sure you have worked out by now that Nick was a client of mine. I'm going to walk you through every step of what he did so you can change jobs, get promoted or do something entirely different into your career. Dig into your reserves of common sense, don't worry about how confident you may or may not feel, just cut all the bull and start focusing on how you can solve other people's problems. Once you have worked this out you will start to feel less vulnerable and more valuable. Employers put the same price tag on you that you put on yourself. You are who you say you are.

Get ready to do some deep thinking.

Zena's Smart Job Search Plan

Mind Flip is about finding low hanging fruit, not wasting hours on fruitless job seeking. Who has a problem that you can solve and what's the simplest way of getting in front of them? Usually the answer is right under your nose. It means picking up the phone, not just responding to job alerts sent to you by an algorithm. It's easy to be a busy job seeker – we all know stories of people complaining they have applied for hundreds of jobs and got nowhere, then blame ageism, sexism, biased recruiters etc. They might have a case, but I think they are confusing efficiency with effectiveness. Their strategy is all action and not much thinking. I'd rather you find something quickly by using your head, so you can sign a contract and then have time to take a well deserved break before you launch yourself into your next career move. Not waste months writing application forms and waiting for the phone to ring. That's what happens when your approach is generic and blunt: your CV and emails go to the 'maybe, might have something in the future' file.

I know some of you will want the reassurance of a process, particularly if you are itching to write a CV and reassure your partner/parents/the nagging voices in your head that you are getting on with it. The process gets increasingly specific and targeted about what you want and where your value lies:

Stage One: Think

1. Think about what you want to do next. It's fine to have several 1
   options; aim for quantity of ideas to start with; practical to
   crazy. Rank them and pick your first option, which will be your
   highest and best use. It will be meaningful
   for you; aligning with your values; and have some element of
   challenge too. This can take a few goes and you might
   change and come back to your really preferred option some
   day in the future.

2. Write down your goals for the job you want next: what it is;
   where; by when; essential criteria; salary, etc. Be as specific as
   possible. Also, write down what you want your work to feel
   like in two years' time, so you will know if you have made the
   right decision.

3. Can you raise the bar on your goals? If you were at the top of
   your game and knew couldn't fail, what would you set your
   mind to? Should you change your goals now to reflect this? If
   not, why not?

4. Define how you are going to sell yourself and your brand.
   Exactly what you do and the problems you solve. Look at the
   competition on LinkedIn. Research keywords and common
   phrases on advertised jobs that you want to apply for, so you
   can mirror the language. What's the difference between a
   brilliant performer and an average one at what you do? Be
   the brilliant one.

5. Work out the gaps in the market for your skillset. Marry up
   what you want to do with client demand.

6. Find proof for how good you are at doing what you do. Back it up with numbers and metrics if you can: percentage improvements; achievement against objectives; achievements against your peers; return on investment; revenues; profits; retention; market share; and employee ratings and so on.

Stage Two: Do

7. Now and only now, write an evidence-based CV and LinkedIn profile using key words and data, aimed at your target market. Is there a better way to reach them, a YouTube clip for example? Write a personal statement that frames who you are and what you can do.

8. Talk to your network and recruiters. Don't do this until you are clear about what you want. You will blow your chances.

9. If it is sensible to do so, post your CV on notice boards and apply for jobs. If you are going down this route, you need to do at least double the activity that you think you have to. Be in multiple processes, five or six at once is fine. Remember that the advertised job market does not reflect the need for your skillset. Companies don't advertise their problems, they don't want to be swamped with CVs and there may already be someone in the post. All reasons why I want you to network, not sit in front of your screen hoping someone calls you back.

10. Network, network and more networking. Get out there and create opportunities. Keep in front of the recruiters. Call every couple of weeks to update them.

11. Interview as much as you can. You are mystery shopping here too, learning as you go. Be in parallel processes if possible, it builds your confidence and gets potential employers feeling they are in a competition to get you.

Stage Three: Review

12. Analyse the patterns in the interest you are getting and do more of what is working. Should you approach competitors of companies that you are interviewing with for example? Rethink your strategy if you aren't getting much interest. Your CV might not be specific enough about the value you offer, your LinkedIn profile might not have enough SEO terms (look at the key words and specialisms you use). Your networking gambit could be vague. I explain more about this in the book.

13. Negotiate objectively and value what you have to offer.

14. When you get a job, set yourself a diary date to review where you are against your career goals. Make sure that the challenges of your new role meet your enhanced and more confident skillset, otherwise you will get bored.

15. Finally, keep nourishing your network to avoid future derailment.

All the help you need to follow this process is in parts one *Figure it out* and two *Crack on*, with extra help for some of you in part three *Just for you*. Life after the successful job search or promotion is in Part Four *Fulfill it*.

Now you know the process, let's start with the biggest question of all: What do you want? You might need to head for a café to do this, to give yourself time and space to figure all this out. Enjoy it because it's not often that we get to ask ourselves these really big questions. Don't worry if the page stays blank for a day or two. Once you start prodding at it your mind will eventually come up with the answers.

Exercise: What do you want?

Step 1. Start the process by working out where you are now. Describe your current career situation and how you feel?

Step 2. Next work out where you want to go. Visualise what you want your working life to look like in the future, being as specific as you can, so you are starting to build in career goals. Imagine it is an ideal world and you can have exactly what you want. What is your job role, job title, location, key role responsibility, rewards, benefits, challenges and who are your team and colleagues?

Step 3. Write everything down as you visualise it.

Step 4. Now, if you knew you were at the top of your game, uniquely qualified, an expert, and you would succeed at what you set out to do, would you raise the bar at all? Update your goal if so.

Step 5. How important is this to you on a scale of 1 – 10?

Step 6. What are the consequences of not achieving this goal?

Step 7. What are the consequences of achieving it?

Step 8. Imagine you are looking back from the future. When have you achieved your goals?

Step 9. What are the actions you took to get there?

Step 10. Start making your plan to put those actions into place. Set your milestones: people to talk to; numbers of meetings to arrange; networking to do; and companies to approach. You need a plan and something to measure your progress against.

Your career goal

Write down, in as much detail as possible, the career move you are looking for. This time you are writing it as a goal to keep you on track.

1

For example, IT Director, by 1 May, minimum salary £120,000, London based, budget about £25m, team of about 50.

Start articulating your answer so you can spread it round your network and answer the: 'What are you looking for? Questions, as the example below.

> *'Having taken a large payoff when Grabbem Smith merged, I have spent the last couple of years doing several personal investment projects, as well as some interim IT transformation roles that came naturally through my network. I am now ready to return to full-time employment and I am looking for an IT Director role within another fee-earning environment, probably a global law or consulting firm with complex IT infrastructure, maybe as a result of acquisitions.'*

Write down this goal somewhere you can see it everyday, to keep you on track. Think of a visual metaphor for achieving this that will keep you motivated: your smart corner office; your delighted global customer; an expensive new wardrobe; the new laptop they buy you; or your achieved financial targets on a spread-sheet. Whatever works for you, maybe an intrinsic reward, which makes you feel good or an extrinsic one, which makes your brother-in-law envious. One of my clients visualised her new business card with her new job title, another pictured the micro-brewery he would start once he'd accumulated the money to start his second, dream, career. Use anything that reminds you of where you want to get to and how it feels when you do.

Congratulations, you've just made a huge leap forward. Now we cross-reference what you want with who wants you. And work out how to get yourself in front of them. We'll start with how a recruiter can help you.

This chapter will show you how to put yourself in a busy recruitment consultant or headhunter's shoes and get them working for you. It will demonstrate how the Recruitment trade works and how to get your CV through their filters.

CHAPTER 3

Be Marmite, not vanilla

These people are critically important to you because the recruitment industry is bigger than ever. The latest figures from the *Recruitment and Employment Confederation's Latest Industry Trends 2015/16* show the value of the recruitment industry to the UK economy was £35.1 billion in 2015, 9 per cent more than the previous year. This is more than the food and beverage industry at £32.6 billion and the advertising and market research industry at £16.9 billion. Clearly, someone is doing something right! Like all professions, there are good and bad but let's assume that if someone has been in the business for a few years they know what they are doing. You are both on the same side – they earn their living by getting you a job.

There are two critical facts often overlooked in the scramble to fire off CVs to agencies and yet, the speed of your job search relies on what you do about them.

Stand Out

Stand out. The recruiter may either love you or hate you but they need to understand what you can do for them and their clients. You want to be in the position of being the obvious solution when there is that gap/opportunity/vacancy. It is vital that you stand out from the rest of the shortlist and be specific about what you do and be able to explain it in a factual and evidence based way. Being generic rarely gets you hired, being specific does. Why should someone hire you?

For example, this does not work.

> *'I am open to opportunities really, where I can use my skills and talents to further my career. What have you got?'*

No recruitment consultant wants to hear that. They have two sections on their database, one for your function, which is your job title and one for your industry or sector. Then there are key words they code you with. No one searches for an 'open to opportunities' category and no one can call their client and say *'I've got a candidate here who is really open to what they do next, they don't mind really, they'll just fit in – we'll charge you ten grand for that please, cheers.'*

You have to spell out exactly what you do and why you do it. For example, this works.

> *'I am a Chief Financial Officer in the insurance sector. I have been on the Board of a Hospital for six years and I now want to use that experience for performance management and governance in the NHS to move into the health sector full time.'*

Be specific

The market for talent is all about specificity. Exactly what do you do, that others don't? What is your expertise? Describe your unique cocktail of experience that culminates in where you are today.

1

Most recruitment is done when someone has left and they need to replace them urgently; not in a succession planning way referred to in the HR textbooks. The situation is usually with a limited time for handovers, person on long-term sick, or we need someone immediately. Or we have a problem or threat or something on the horizon we need to deal with and we want a specialist to handle it. I want to send them an email, get them to deal with it and get back to the rest of my inbox. I want to hire a candidate who makes me look good. Or at the very least who isn't going to get me fired because they were such a random hire that they were too much of a risk in the first place.

Be the Cookie Cutter

Hiring managers don't say 'let's get the cheapest person in' either. They want the best possible person for their budget and their budgets are stretched considerably if they think they are getting competitive talent in. By best, they mean a cookie-cutter image of their last person; only more perfect because the last person must have been flawed otherwise they wouldn't have left the company, right? You need to be that cookie cutter image and prove you can hit the ground running.

I tell my clients to put their necks on the line and make sure their application is very specific about what they can do. There is still a chance that a safe, vague, generic application will get them an interview, particularly if they have a great CV or come from a competitor, or an organisation with a reputation for hiring talent. They could even get quite far down the interview process. However, more often than not, the feedback is inevitably along the lines of "yes, they really liked you, but they have gone for someone with a bit more relevant experience of.. etc." It can be very frustrating, but stick to Mind flipping for the solution.

The best way forward is to decide what you want to do next and what your expertise is, back it up with proof, throw the kitchen sink at getting it and if it doesn't work, then revise and try again.

The other important fact about the recruitment industry is the 3.5 seconds it takes to 'read' your CV. Here's what frustrated recruiters want you to know.

Order your CV

The other important fact to know about the recruitment industry is that it only takes them 3.5 seconds to 'read' your CV. It is the relevance of your most recent experience that counts the most because this is what employers will read first. If you only remember one key message from this entire book, please make it this one.

The last job on your CV is the most important.

If it's not relevant, recruiters discard it. Ping, delete, gone.

Here is the order most people who regularly screen CVs approach the document on their screen.

- Name
- Address (quick scan – how far do you have to travel)
- Most recent job
- Job title
- Most recent employer (is it a good employer brand)
- Details (achievements)
- Back up to the personal statement section (if they like what they read so far)
- Previous roles
- Education, qualifications (possibly earlier if this crucial to the job spec, as in technical or IT roles)
- Hobbies (maybe, if they are eye catching and enhance your brand)

This is what they consider you to be: the job title and role responsibility you describe as your current or most recent job. Make sure how you write your CV as relevant to the reader. You have to get through the filtering processes and the person screening your CV is usually the bottom of the pile in the recruitment consultancy or the junior person in the resourcing team. They have been told to 'go through all 300 CVs and show us the top 20 who match these criteria… they have to have done the job before in a similar environment.' If your job title doesn't match and the keywords don't correlate, they won't realise you are a good fit for the role and they won't keep reading. It's the same for your LinkedIn profile too.

1

There are some tricks that might help you fiddle around with this and make your CV more relevant. There is more information in Chapter 10: *CVs and LinkedIn; Why are you telling them this?*

- Change your work experience to emphasise the most relevant information that matches the 'responsibilities of the role' at the beginning of the job description, but not every single competency. Don't tell them everything you have ever done. Just show how you match the role requirements. They don't need to know how great you are at stuffing envelopes unless you want to be Chief Envelope Stuffer next time.

For example below is an example, of someone who truthfully but judiciously, tweaking his current work experience to suit the role he wanted.

'At 22, Peter was hired to drive a van for a company that archived film and videos for TV production companies. He was a fun person, popular with customers. When he wasn't busy driving or working in the warehouse, his manager got him to do some telephone and administrative work in the office, managing client queries and orders and using the

CRM system. When the time came to leave he was able to use this experience to move on. He called his job Customer Services/Administration on his CV and mentioned the driving aspect in the final bullet point of his role description. He described his business as media rather than storage because that's the sector he was servicing, even if technically he worked in the storage industry. He understood the structure, problems and needs of media production companies. The recruiters who contacted him would never have approached him if he said he was a Driver in a Warehouse.'

- Match your job title to the specifications. If you are really a Project Manager but your current job title is something unique to your organisation – a Customer Workflow Manager for example – then call yourself Project (Customer Workflow) Manager, or Project/Workflow Manager - whatever is most sensible. Explain what you have done and why at interview, but don't make it a big deal. Obviously, I am not suggesting you should pretend to be something you're not. But make it obvious what you are because the person reading your CV isn't paid to figure it out. They average another 299 CVs for each job and they are keen to cull as many as possible.

- If your voluntary, part-time or extra curricular experience is more relevant than your day job to what you want to do next, put that as the most recent job. It is irrelevant if you aren't paid. It is fine to have more than one current role. You can explain all this in your personal statement.

- If you have worked in a succession of different roles for the same employer you don't need to break the CV down with each one. July 2013 – March 2014, April 2015 – May 2016 and so on. The CV isn't everything you have ever done in your life, it's supposed to be a marketing document that gets you an interview for the job you want next. Say something like 'joined as a Junior Account

Manager in 2009, consistently promoted through the ranks to reach Senior Client Manager in June 2016.' Pick out relevant achievements and put the most relevant ones at the top, even if they aren't the most current.

1

Your CV; your voice

There is no right or wrong way to write a CV. If it is getting you interviews then it is working. It doesn't matter if you deliver a cake with your phone number iced on it, if that gets you in the door.

I don't like CVs and long for the day when we can use LinkedIn profiles or an equivalent and a Youtube CV or a SoundCloud account with podcasts. I'm sure it's not far away. I save my venom though for the homogenised CVs that are written by many professional CV writers, which send my bull detector into orbit. I know I am not alone in this among the recruitment community. Invariably, they hype up experience to the extent that the person seems over qualified for the work they want to get. When you interview the candidate, you know at the handshake stage when the candidate hasn't written it themselves and the CV doesn't accurately represent the person - sorry, innovative thought-leader - sitting in front of you. Getting your CV written for you is an option, if you are applying for jobs in a different language, otherwise I would question why someone else can write about something you should feel passionate about: you and what you do for others. If you don't feel that passion, then that's an indicator you should be doing something different.

The filtering process; why key words are so important

When I was a recruiter's recruiter, we used to headhunt estate agents from one particular firm, renowned for hiring good calibre graduates, to convince them to move into the recruitment industry and work for our clients instead. They might have had to lose the cute minis they drove, but the basic salaries were better and they wouldn't have to work on weekends. When we did persuade them, they started off as either researchers in headhunting firms or resources in recruitment agencies, particularly IT recruitment agencies which were booming at the time. These guys had been pushing up the price of flats one week and scrutinising CVs the next, with fairly limited training or understanding of the positions they were working on.

The system hasn't changed: in fact now with the deluge of CVs hitting recruiters daily from all round the world our raw graduate can even be replaced by a robot – an applicant tracking system. So the CV you have spent days developing can be eliminated simply because you didn't use the right key words that match the requirements and the recruiter - let's call him Charlie - let your genius pass him by.

How to get past Charlie

Start the CV writing process by finding jobs you really want to apply for. The aggregator www.indeed.co.uk is a good place to start. Print them, take a highlighter and find phrases and words that keep coming up. Put these into your own document and LinkedIn profile. Most job ads have been copied from someone elses and you will see patterns emerge. Make sure your language matches their language and you are putting in all the details they are looking for. Obvious ones are particular requirements of the job. Work backwards. If you were briefing Charlie on the criteria you would expect to see on a CV, what would you tell him to look out for?

'I need a System Administrator to work at FrenchCorp. I only want to see CVs that show someone has a minimum of three years' experience as a Systems Administrator probably no more than five or else they will be too senior. They should have worked with more than 50 users. They need a BSc in computer science – maybe web technology - or network administration or something similar. They must show proof of certification so Cisco Certified Network Associate or Cisco Certified Network Professional. I also need them to

1

have Sun Solaris certifications, Microsoft Certified System Administrator and Red Hat RHCT because they will use Linux. If they don't have all of that, don't bother. It's a French company so it would be handy if they had fluent French. If they haven't already worked in telephone companies they should have worked somewhere else that is regulated and mention regulation or compliance. The company is upgrading the system so they should mention they have been involved in an upgrade and show success in that. They are working with non techies so look for a mention of their good communication skills and smooth relationships with users, something about internal customers, understanding of the business requirements, strategy or stakeholder management. FrenchCorp is a tough place to work so I want to see numbers and targets; achievement against target, user satisfaction rates, speed of upgrade, key performance indicators and solid evidence that they have worked in a performance driven environment.'

Note that at no stage are personality traits mentioned. Charlie then passes the CV to the recruiter he works for who deals with the client. The client though isn't usually the IT Manager. It's likely to be another Charlie in the client's HR or internal resourcing department who passes it upwards. Or even a Charlie in another recruitment agency, acting in a master vendor role, managing other recruitment suppliers. At each stage your CV gets filtered. Most of the communication is online so no one is talking to anyone else about what a perfect fit you are. You are ringing your Charlie to find out what's going on and the reality is he often has no feedback because he hasn't heard back either. You are lost in a process somewhere. It might be that he isn't even working for a preferred supplier to FrenchCorp his agency might be a secondary supplier trying to get through with a lucky CV. Charlie wishes he was back in estate agency where at least he was meeting real people, not at a desk wearing headphones and having you complaining that you haven't heard anything.

You can see the frustration.

The upshot is that Mr Client needs a System Administrator now. He can't wait for his HR department to come up with good CVs so he offers the job to the contractor already in his department who is not brilliant but is the quickest option and the devil he knows.

You hear no feedback or get the message that they offered it internally. You get despondent because you think the whole thing was a waste of time. Or, you are falsely optimistic that FrenchCorp have your CV on their internal talent register and will contact you, through Charlie, about other similar roles. This is unlikely. Charlie's boss leaves and goes to a competitor, who gets the business and takes the relationship with FrenchCorp. Or your CV never actually got to FrenchCorp, anyway.

You may have been overlooked or not got through the Charlie filter because you might have been educated in Chad and speak great French but that seems so obvious to you didn't mention it. Charlie is looking for the word 'French.' Or If you had just 18 months experience, but could do a great job, you won't get through the process because the agency has been told exactly the criteria they need to match. They don't have the relationship with the client, or the communication channel to risk CVs that don't match exactly. They fear getting chucked off the preferred supplier list if they do. There are 100s of other agencies who want the client's business. So, the employer suffers from missing out on high potential talent.

I am using broad-brush strokes to drive home my point. But whatever level you are at, you have to actively match those requirements and stand out. Some recruiters have very special relationships and work differently of course.

Find the back door

Of course, you have to use recruitment agencies and third parties like this as part of your job search. It's a £28 billion industry so that's a lot of people placed in jobs every year. But also use your network and be that internal candidate. Where are your previous colleagues and managers working? Find them and network into organisations directly so you are there when the jobs come up. Get in as a consultant, contractor or interim if you are available. And make sure your CV is crammed with all the key words and phrases so you stand out as the best of the long list, then the short list.

If you are something straightforward like a Systems Integrator it is fairly easy to find a new role, particularly if you are staying in the same industry. You are staying in the same function in the same sector. Recruiters like this, they aren't paid to find someone who hasn't actually done the job but could be really good at it. That's a quick way to upset their client. They are paid to find someone who can hit the ground running.

You can change sector or function but rarely both at once, unless someone knows you and gives you a chance. If you are changing sectors then spell out the similarities between what you have done in the past and what you want to do next. Join the dots for them. Don't expect them to work it out.

Here's an example of someone switching sectors.

'Clare was an Organisational Psychologist working for a trade union. She had been applying for jobs in management consulting but recruiters weren't shortlisting her because at first glimpse of her CV they immediately thought she wasn't the right cultural fit – more of a left-wing, right-on union character than a hard nosed corporate person. Clare rewrote her CV to show that a big part of her trade union role was working with FTSE 100 companies on their employee relations strategy and she named and placed

1

these organisations so they really caught the readers eye. Recruiters realised that she was the type of person they could introduce to these clients because she was already comfortable in that type of professional context. She got a job in a top organisational consulting firm, with unionised clients who needed a Psychologist with particular knowledge of how trade unions worked.'

Unclear what your expertise is?

If you are still unsure about what you want to do next, or what you want to highlight to recruiters – or maybe you are considering several options – her is an exercise to help you.

Soapbox Exercise: What are you going to talk about?

In five minutes you are going to stand outside your office/house/building and talk for two minutes on a subject that you feel passionate and knowledgeable about.

- Will it be about whatever you were doing when you were most engaged at work?
- Or has your expertise evolved since then?
- What comes into your mind immediately?

That is likely to be the area where you have most expertise. If it's not work related then make a note of it and think of another example from work. You may have more than one obvious career option but go with the one that makes you feel most energised when you think about it. Many of my clients have gone back in their later careers to what they enjoyed doing when they were in their late teens – writing, shop-keeping, chutney making etc. - perhaps not full time, but as portfolio or investment or retirement options.

1

Imagine you are giving your presentation and answer these questions.

What is the title of your talk?
- I have to tweet about it, so you need to give me a snappy title.

Who is your audience?
- I can rent any crowd you like, so who do you want to listen to you?
- What do they look like/have in common?
- What problems might they have?
- What do they need from you?
- What keeps them awake at night?

Why does your presentation matter to them?
- What do they get out of it?
- What problems does it solve for them?
- How will they be different after hearing your presentation?
- What is the benefit to them?

Why does it matter to you?
- Where is the meaning in this for you?
- Why is it important to you that this particular group benefits from your expertise?

Does this help you drill down into what you want to do next, the people you want to work with and where your work has most meaning? This is your area of expertise and what some people call your personal brand or work identity.

Last word about recruiters

Remember they are not paid to be your friend. There was a time, pre-internet, when you met recruiters and got to know them well. These days, whatever level you are at, they will only meet you if they think you are suitable for their clients or are right for a particular role. Or, if they want to build a relationship with you because they think you could be a potential client of theirs in the future. Don't take it personally. These are sales people and you want them working for you, hustling to get vacancies, not wasting time chatting to candidates.

If you do meet them and even when you talk to them on the phone, stay on your guard. If they invite you in for a chat, they will be weighing you up to see if they can put you in front of their clients. Have a strong story to sell, including your future ambitions. Look and behave like you could be on site at their best client's offices. Trust your instincts if you can share more personal information with them, for example that in an ideal world you would prefer not to work five days a week. Leave them a really clear message about who you are and what you do, so they remember who you are when they look at your CV a month later, to finally file you on their database. It helps to send a follow-up email summarising your discussion that they could cut and paste to send out to clients with your CV.

Most recruitment consultants will make sure their colleagues know about you if they work in different industry sectors that might also be relevant to you. Don't assume this. I find that boutique search firms are less efficient than larger agencies with more formal processes. It partly depends on whether they get a percentage of an introduction fee, or if they operate in stand-alone silos. For example, if you have a good relationship with the permanent consultant it doesn't mean they will automatically introduce you to the person who deals with contract or temporary roles. Possibly because they don't want you to be tied up in a contract so you won't be able to start their job immediately. Ask if you can also talk to their colleagues. You may register with a head office but would also consider a local role so a chat to their regional office would be useful. Again, do this yourself. Never assume that once you are on the database your work is done.

1

When you find your next role, maintain contact with helpful recruiters. Continue to invest in the relationship so you have their support when you need it. Take their calls, give them tip-offs about vacancies if you can, talk to them about what is going on in your sector, give them names of people who might be suitable for roles if you aren't interested. I know great head hunters who return the favour by helping their candidates to negotiate offers, even when they haven't made the introduction.

Obviously, there are many who merely unsubtly probe you for leads and you might want to keep them at arm's lengths. In several sectors these pushy ones can be quite successful, so don't burn your bridges with them. But equally well, don't feel under pressure to tell them about other vacancies you have been approached about.

> 'I've been asked not to reveal who it is at this stage. But, of course I'll tell you just as soon as I can. Now, do you have anything specific for me – what I am looking for is …?'

It can be frustrating and demoralising to be screened by a youngster with very little insight into what you do. Grit your teeth and be polite, you need to get up the chain to speak to someone more experienced. Give them all the key words they need to understand you and refer you upwards. You only need one vacancy and sometimes these agencies are the ones who get lucky. The morality and fairness of this process is another conversation.

Exercise: Why you?

Answer these questions or draw a Mind Map, to help you be really clear about what you have to offer.

- Why should someone hire you?
- What do you do better and differently from your peers or competitors?

1

This chapter will demonstrate that the fastest way to find a new job is to stop looking for one; instead create opportunities for yourself.

CHAPTER 4

Create your own opportunities

When you are a job seeker it would seem pretty logical to go looking for a job. Well, yes, that's the end goal, but switch your mindset. Get out there and look for problems you can solve and create opportunities for yourself. Don't wait for an advertised job - that's one way - but it's the slow way. It's reckoned that only 20% of jobs are advertised these days anyway, not all sectors are legally obliged to advertise their vacancies. It adds to their workload and can damage their brand with customers if they apply for jobs and don't get them. By all means apply for jobs, but work through your network and your network's network. This is what people call 'the hidden job market'.

Many people approach job seeking in the same way they approach their everyday job. This means they are so focused on doing everything by the book that they miss leftfield or easy opportunities right under their nose. Yes, lawyers and accountants, I mean you. Simplify the process; look for low hanging fruit.

What your Auntie will tell you to do and why it's wrong

The 'new' traditional way that people seem to fall into is to spend hours and hours preparing their CV, a generic one that appeals to lots of different job ads, register on half a dozen job boards, send off CVs to loads of agencies and spend days in front of their computer responding to job alerts and making applications. This certainly keeps them busy and it might work. But most likely it won't work and they will feel frustrated and demotivated. They won't get any feedback at all. No agency will want to meet them, but they may well get some calls from people offering to rewrite their CV or help them tap into the 'hidden job market.' It will also take far too long.

You've already discovered a better process plan in Chapter 2: *It's not About You; Zena's Smart Job Search Plan*. Here's the rationale for why following it will help you get better work more quickly, be it, permanent, temporary, freelance: it's the same process more quickly:

Smart thinking precedes smart talking

Like most areas of life, the quality of your thinking makes the difference between an average move and a brilliant one. You need a targeted job search, so first be clear on exactly what that target is. Although it is counter intuitive, the aim is to have a small target market with only a few opportunities, which clearly need your unique set of skills.

For example, if you are a town planner specialising in bio-diverse urban environments in multi-cultural communities, find the consultancies that work in that space and approach them. You only need one job! Generic job seeking approaches and keeping your options open won't work in this market. You have to be very specific about the problems you can solve and why you are better and different to the competition. You can always revisit this and change tack. The main thing is to be active and experiment and take risks. Throw the kitchen sink at finding your ideal next move and set yourself a deadline. If there really is no desire for your services, or no market for those skills, or perhaps after a while you decide that's not really what you want to do, then change. It is far better to adopt this approach than being half-hearted. Inertia is no help in a job search; take control.

Develop an action habit. Think. Do. Revise.

Back up your CV and LinkedIn profile with hard achievements

I am not a big fan of relying on CVs for your job search, as you will have spotted by now. I'd far rather you picked up the phone to call your network. However, you are obviously going to need one at some stage, at the very least for your new HR department to file. So, it is helpful to get hard evidence about your expertise down on paper now, not least because this is a useful exercise to think through your previous achievements. There is more detail about CVs in: *CVs and LinkedIn; Why are you telling them this?* The most important point being that the CV is a selling document to show that you have nailed the problems your potential employer wants you to solve. It is not a list of everything you have ever done in your working life. Recruiters don't care about that. They want to know how they can save or – better still – make money if they hire you and the proof of that is what you have already learnt on someone else's payroll). They want to know what you can do for them and they want to see you demonstrate success at it. I am repeating this message I know – I'll keep doing it throughout the book, because this is what *Mind Flip* is all about.

Do much more than you think you need to

Many people who find work quickly do far more activity to find it than people who don't. That's it. They are prepared to stick their neck out, risk rejection and approach the job market like their day job. Aim for at least 60 different job search activities to get work.

For example:
- send out a CV
- apply for a job
- contact recruiters
- ask for LinkedIn connections
- attend events
- meet people for coffee
- attend job interviews
- make direct applications
- and do much more.

A job seeking activity is anything related to getting you work. Don't worry about having too much on the go at once. You will be amazed at how your dead certs will drop off your list and how your pipeline will change from week to week. Put your number on your LinkedIn profile and CV and make it easy for people to get hold of you. I have never yet had a client overwhelmed by calls from recruiters, interviews or job offers. It's a problem I'd love to deal with.

Throw the kitchen sink at getting what you want. Do two or three times more activities than you think are necessary. It's not quite a full time job finding work, but if you are out of a job and trying to find a new one, you should spend about three days a week on it, or five half days. The rest of the time you spend on positive activities to keep your spirits up. I like my clients to commit to a project where they actually can see an end result – they have done all sorts of things from taking up welding, making a wooden framed garage and open water swimming, to mastering Victoria sponges. Anything that makes them feel good; teaches them a new skill; keeps up the energy levels; and gets them away from their screen. I have noticed that they do much better at interview when they are feeling good about themselves and are less stressed. Desperation is never attractive.

Cover the bases with digital job seeking

Make sure you are visible. If you are out of work and actively on the market, post your CV on job boards, perhaps two generic ones and two specialist one for the role you do or the sector you are in. Experiment with three or four and see which one works for you. If you get agencies contacting you for the wrong type of job, or inappropriate roles suggested to you, then that tells you your filters are incorrect or you haven't optimised your CV with the right key words. Recruiters want to find you, rather than feel that every other consultancy is sending you round the market too.

A warning about job alerts

These are the mother of all time wasters. Firstly, you do not have to apply for a job alert that is emailed to you directly. It's not a nice person sending it to you it's just an algorithm. Secondly, it is a huge, depressing time-waster. At best, if it's wrong, it shows you that your key words aren't correctly optimised.

Back away from that screen

You've ticked the boxes for digital job seeking. Now get away from your computer screen. You won't find a great job by hiding behind it, tempting though it is. If you are relying on advertised roles all you are doing is staying in the swamp with everyone else. Get out there and talk to people: existing people and new people; about what you can do for them.

You have to hustle a bit and ask for what you want. Create your own opportunities and take control. Remember that as well as finding work, you are trying to build a network so you are never derailed in the future. People who you meet now might be useful to you at a later stage. Put credit in the bank. And if you aren't right for their business, they might be able to refer you to people who are. It all helps to reinforce your personal brand. They might actually be nice people anyway.

Keep scanning the business newsfeeds. As recruiters we want to work with successful organisations who are growing, but we also want clients with problems and we look for good candidates who can make a sustainable difference to them at the same time as enhancing their own future career prospects. We don't want to recruit for organisations who are static; bumping along. We only use those as a source to headhunt frustrated employees. Know who are the noisier, growing firms in your sector and who has the problems. Identify who is losing contracts or accreditations, has falling profits, missed forecast, pulled out of new markets and has high-profile leavers or poor PR. They need you.

Talking to people about what you can do for them will help you to uncover the mysterious hidden job market; unadvertised roles. My clients get jobs created for them by going out and talking to people about their business problems and skilfully suggesting how they can help solve them.

Reach out to them. I'm sure you've heard the joke that unless you are actually in The Four Tops you should never actually use that expression! Do this in the most appropriate way; phone, direct email, networks, recruitment consultancy, Twitter, nobbling them at conferences and build relationships on Instagram. Do this in a way that most reflects your brand and the way you work. For example, if you are in sales, then pick up the phone. If you are a designer, send them an example of your designs.

Here are a couple of examples for you.

> *Marco was Head of Procurement for a global food manufacturing business, let's call it Beanz Inc. and part of his job was evaluating bids from smaller companies who wanted to supply ingredients. When he left Beanz, he contacted some of these suppliers and said he could help them improve their bid process, obviously without revealing confidential Beanz information. It's the classic, Zena's Poacher*

Turned Gamekeeper Move. How could they say no? He met with several, chose one, started as a consultant helping them with bids and tenders, moved onto making performance improvements in the procurement department itself and ended up taking a leadership role across the whole buying and procurement division.

Sally also worked for Beanz, setting up two overseas manufacturing units for them. Once these were in place, she returned to the Dutch head office in a broader management role. Happiest when out in the field, building something from scratch, she quickly became bored. She scanned the press and talked to several headhunters but there weren't any roles that appealed to her. She read about a competitor's safety problems with one of their international operations, sent an email directly to the COO and said she might be able to help. They had several meetings and she was hired into a new role, created for her.

Use Glassdoor online

Glassdoor is an exciting new website where current and former employees review companies and their management. It's the Trip Advisor/Trust Pilot equivalent for the recruitment industry. Use it to check out potential employers and understand their culture. Remember, like Trip Advisor not all reviews are true or unbiased. Poor reviews create opportunities too. The organisation needs to change and needs new fresh blood to help it do that. If less foresighted candidates might be put off joining an organisation, that means you can benefit from reduced competition. Glassdoor helps you understand problems and know the right questions to ask at interview. As is the philosophy of this book, assume nothing and get your own proof rather than hearsay. Check it out here: www.glassdoor.co.uk

Relish rejection

Go to as many interviews as you can. I recommend that you
need to be in at least ten interview processes to get a job and
of course this varies according to your seniority and industry.
The more rejections you have, statistically the closer you are to
getting hired. See rejection as a positive learning experience.
Like notches on your bedpost to find the partner that's right
for you.

Learn from any feedback you get and analyse your own
performance to see how you can improve. When you get invited
to an interview go, at least for the practice obviously checking
that the salary is roughly in your ballpark first. You can only take
one job. If you are interviewing with potential competitors then
treat it like a mystery shopping exercise. Gather information, as
they are doing about you. Think about the following questions.

- How does this organisation sell themselves to you and to
  their marketplace?
- What can you learn that will help you shine in your
  next job?
- What does this tell me about trends and best practice in
  your industry to keep current.
- Make as many connections as possible, for later.

Use your own best instincts

Just because someone tells you how they found their next job
it doesn't mean that process will necessarily work for you. They
might be a civil servant and you work in advertising. These
are two entirely different career paths and obviously have two
entirely different ways of changing roles. The first one will rely
on application forms for advertised roles on websites, such as
www.jobsgopublic.com Although, I know there are plenty of
people who network into consulting roles in the public sector.
The second career path, definitely involves engaging with
people via digital marketing channels and social media. Both of

these methods reflect the competencies you need to do your job effectively – the first is diligent form filling - the second is understanding your target market and reaching out to them effectively. Take all the advice you are given, but filter it with a heavy dose of common sense.

Are there any cheeky short cuts?

What's under your nose? Many of my clients go back to work for previous employers, the second or third last jobs on their CVs, either working for their old bosses in a new organisation or the companies they have previously worked for and left. HR departments like to rehire employees. It's a great message for the rest of the staff. *'Jess worked for us, thought the grass was greener, but it's actually not: look, she's come back to us.'* Also, Jess will have acquired new skills and knowledge from a competitor, which will benefit her old organisation. This is another reason why it is important to be a good leaver; you never know when you want to go back. It's not a career pattern you want to get in the habit of, but I think you can get away with going back at least once.

Recruiters can get nervous when taking references for exactly this reason. If they talk directly to the person you worked for, who finds out that you are on the market, it is not uncommon for them to pick up the phone to try and persuade you to come back. It's not uncommon for the recruiter to try and place you with a previous employer either: on the basis that they wouldn't have known you were on the market otherwise. If I was that employer, I'd think it was strange that you hadn't picked up the phone and contacted me directly, even if it was under the guise of discreetly picking my brains on the market.

Even cheekier, I have also seen people go back to the organisation that made them redundant, perhaps as a contractor or consultant. Often, the best employees leave in voluntary redundancy processes. They have confidence in their abilities and know they can find a new role elsewhere and they decide to take the money. The business loses valuable skills and has short-term talent problems, so HR swallows its pride, gets the chequebook out and invites them to come back. Previous colleagues with less chutzpah may not be very welcoming, but they are filling a commercial need.

Zena's Poacher Turned Gamekeeper Move

Who needs you as a direct consequence of where you are working now? Think about your competitors, suppliers and customers? I had a client who had worked in magazine publishing, then had a spell in PR. She wanted a corporate career and got hired by the communications department of one of her clients. As well as her obvious communications expertise, they wanted her knowledge of how journalists and PR consultants work because she would now be on the other side of the desk, as the client feeding them the messages she wanted published. She now knows the dark arts of PR so is a much more effective client. Who has a vested interest in keeping you in the market: your auditors; lawyers; headhunters; stakeholders; and anyone who will get more business from you, if you are in a new role?

It's also worth bearing in mind that some organisations pay a bounty or referral fee if someone recommends you. Your mate could get up to several thousand pounds if you join his organisation and pass probation. It saves on agency fees and you are more likely to be a successful hire if you already understand the culture and have contacts and friends in the company. Don't feel that your friends are being kind by passing on your CV - they are - but they may also benefit financially, so don't be frightened to ask for favours.

Right, so, where's the obvious, quickest way for you to find work? Rather than a large network, people often have one or two sponsors to help them – often people who they have worked for in the past, who still have a benevolent interest in them - can refer them to their networks. Who are yours? If you haven't got these relationships, start building them now for next time.

1

You can't always control the outcome of your activities, but you can control your time and what you do with it. From now on what you believe about your ability to add value - bullfighting not bull-talking - will determine how successful you are at finding better work more quickly.

The rest of this book will tell you how to manage all the separate components of doing this.

Exercise: State the obvious

Answer these questions in depth and write down or Mind Map your answers.
- What's right under your nose?
- What's the quickest route to market for you?
- Who should you be talking to, who you haven't approached yet?

This chapter will explore what to do when you want to do something different but can't work out your transferable skills. It will show you a great career decision-making pathway, which is called, the science of the gut.

'Many career theorists have argued that a career is no more or less than a series of decisions and interpretations.'

Tiederman, O'Hara and Baruch, 1963

CHAPTER 5

Skillset audit

We construct our careers and our working identity through our interpretation of what we do and the perceived meaning it brings to us. Mind Flip changes our focus away from ourselves and on to the value we bring to other people. We then feel more valuable and therefore more empowered and confident. This is reflected back in how other people perceive us, so we get and keep even better work.

Gut factor is important in making career decisions. I've noticed my clients approach their careers in the way they have trained in their day jobs. If they focus on detail, they worry about the detail of their own career. If they are trained to think strategically, they think more broadly about their career options. However, no matter how rational and informed their decisions appear to be, in reality decisions are strongly fielded by emotion (Kidd, 2004). We have a gut instinct as to the decision we should take, which we then intellectualise. How we develop that gut instinct is usually a combination of our values – what is most important to us and our moral compass - and then practical experimentation. When you want to make a career decision, pay attention to what your gut instinct is telling you to do.

Is a gradual or a radical change right for you?

Job search is much easier if you are making a lateral move - a similar/slightly more senior role - in the same sector. That's exactly what recruiters are paid to do - to find someone with proven experience - who can hit the ground running and make an immediate impact.

Of course, not everyone wants to tread the same path; some people want to change sectors or roles or do something entirely different. This is a bit harder to do and the opportunities are far more likely to come from networking rather than a third party recruiter. Many experts predict that people entering the job market today will have an average of seven career changes, although there is detailed debate about what exactly a career change means. For many of us 'change' isn't drastically different, we just take the skills and experience we have acquired so far and gradually build on them, reinventing ourselves every time. In my own career, I have used my recruiter's knowledge of interviewing and fitting people into jobs to switch to working on the candidate side as a career coach, then doing far more executive coaching, then speaking on careers issues and now writing.

An apt metaphor for incremental career change is Tarzan swinging from tree to tree; we accumulate knowledge on the way and leave out-dated skills behind us as we grow and develop. These transitions are the result of trial and error and incremental experience; more of a crooked journey than a jagged path. They may be created by our own desire to improve or change, or may be forced on us by external events such as redundancies, burnout or insufferable working environments.

The radical route

Radical career changers, who end up in a totally different place, construct their path over many years. They might try a few different jobs in their twenties, think they've found their purpose in their thirties, change their mind in their forties and experiment

1

a little to find something they want to do in their fifties, trying out and rejecting lots of options on the way. Despite the media stories, it is rare that people do something completely different overnight - from Business Analyst - to Baker for example. They will have been baking and selling cakes on the side for many years before making the final leap.

In *How To Find Fulfilling Work* Roman Krznaric compares two types of career change experimentation: the branching project and the radical sabbatical. The branching project is the less risky option, where you conduct small experiments around the sides of your existing career. Here is an example.

Maggie was an Accountant who loved cooking and entertaining. She started a part-time events business and slowly started to get commissions for weekend wedding receptions and parties. Eventually, she reduced her hours until, several years later she quit altogether, confident she had enough local reputation and a business pipeline to make a good living. Her training as an accountant made her cautious enough not to do anything drastic.

The radical sabbatical is what Krznaric describes as a job holiday - taking a few month of unpaid leave - or using a couple of weeks holiday to trial something different. Is that grass always greener? Sometimes a compromise is good enough: changing to a job that involves more travel rather than being stuck in the office all the time might satisfy your need for freedom, rather than chucking in the towel altogether and retraining. You actually don't know what's right for you until you try things out. Counter intuitively action is more important than planning at this stage.

In her seminal book on career transitions *Working Identity* Herminia Ibarra writes that the logical process to a successful career change is knowing what we want to do next and using that knowledge to guide our actions. In fact, change happens the other way round: doing comes first, knowing second. If we try and think our way through career change we get stuck. It's better to gradually be exposed to new roles, relationships and responsibilities and our working identity - how we see ourselves in our professional capacity - will catch up. Otherwise, reinventing our professional capacity, how we see ourselves and how we want the rest of the world to see us, is too daunting and we remain where we are.

'Career transitions follow a first-act-and-then-think-sequence.'

Herminia Ibarra, 2003

When you want to change your work and therefore your working identity, the emphasis is on action; doing things, seeing if you enjoy them and relishing the U turns as you learn through practice. It can be a branching project, or a radical sabbatical or exploring options and developing new skills. Whatever it is, crack on and do it. Rigid planning at any stage can lead to inertia: that book we never write because we are waiting for a good time to start. It is almost impossible to execute a career reinvention in a planned and orderly way because no amount of self-reflection can substitute for actual experimentation. It helps to know what you are bringing with you: the transferable skills and expertise that help you segue from one role to something different.

Dear parents, bite your tongue if your child keeps starting, stopping and changing jobs in the early years of their career. It's better that they do this, than be stuck in something miserable, internalise that misery and stop taking action. As long as they are moving forward and will recognise they are in the right role when they find it, everything is going to be fine. Help them to construct a helpful narrative that puts a positive spin on their moves by explaining the skills they have accumulated.

1

When coaching clients through a career transition, I work on the gap between where you are now and where you want to be. Instead of being too prescriptive about the end point, you explore how you want to feel when you get there. Then you can explore different options, knowing how you will recognise when you have made a decision on what is 'best' for you. If you are too prescriptive, i.e. rigid about options, you can miss out on golden opportunities because they weren't in your plan.

These are some of the questions to ask yourself.

- How do I feel now about my working life?
- What are the consequences of not making a change?
- How will I know when I have made the right decision and chosen the right option for me?
- How will I feel about my work then?
- What are my values and how should my work more closely align to my values in the future?
- If I was doing the right kind of work for me, what difference would other people notice about me? How could they tell I had made the right decision?

This type of thinking gives you a navigation point, so you know what the end result is going to feel like although you don't know the exact destination. Then you have to work out what all the options are and experiment with them. If you can't pinpoint all the options, then I go into more depth to work out the 'hooks' that help you switch from one role to another: your transferable skills. These are the skills, experience and networks, which help you switch sectors or do something different.

How do you work out your transferable skills?

I use this exercise to help my clients work out their skillset; their functional and sector expertise and everything they know about. We end up with a breakdown of their unique skillset, or personal brand, which will give then some ideas of what they should do next and where to start looking for opportunities.

You may feel uncomfortable about being an 'expert'. My definition of expertise is that you know more about a subject than the other person. No one is saying you need to have a PhD on the subject, just that you know more than the others. Usually it's the unique blend of experience that makes up your skillset and which makes you marketable; expertise about particular subjects in particular contexts. This is what we dig into here. This might sound flippant, I assume throughout the book that you are who you say you are, you aren't making up your skillset and that we are operating on a base of integrity.

The audit starts with the functional/sector segmentation that is found in recruitment and search firms. This is how candidates are saved on recruiter's databases. Firstly, we know their function (job title or profession: accountant, social worker or project manager etc.) and secondly, their sector (the sector they work in now, or they want to work in next: financial services, third sector, or pharmaceutical etc.).

Of course, your function and sector are the tip of the iceberg, there is so much more to each of us than these two aspects. Our real personal brand comes from the third column: the combination of knowledge, experience, cultural background, thinking styles, organisational context and networks that makes us suited to particular opportunities. Recruiters dig into this to find the pearls that differentiate the best candidate for the job.

This is how you break down your skillset, in the way a clever recruiter would. It is the best way to get right under the bonnet to find out exactly what you know about and who you know.

Take three blank A4 pages, a whole one for each of the three columns you need so you can brain storm as much information as possible. We are looking for patterns and hopefully eureka moments too. Enjoy this exercise. You will find you know much more than you thought.

Skillset Audit
Column One: Functional Experience
This is exactly what you do. What is your job title; chartered accountant, personal assistant, corporate lawyer, shipping agent, veterinary assistant, marketing director, or project manager, etc. Your last job title might be unique to your organisation. What does a Customer Relationship Executive or Leader of Values actually do? Or a sales/customer service/project management, or what? Translate your title into the more regularly used version. Make some notes here about what you do. Who are your customers. What do you project manage? What kind of relationships do you supervise?

1

Write down exactly what your job involves in the way you would describe it to your grandmother. That's taken from an old City interviewing question; patronising but it makes the point.

When people start to job search, they often start by keeping their options open and their search generic *'I can do anything really – what do you need?'* For example, if they have worked as a Financial Director in an Investment Bank, then they think they can be a Financial Director anywhere.

The reality is that although this may be the case, it isn't easy to move sectors and usually recruiters are asked to supply candidates who are already in a similar context doing a very similar role. That's why we are digging deep here into specifics – exactly what you do and where you do it. We are aiming for marmite here – you will be the clear candidate for some jobs and too specialist for others.

Column Two: Sector Experience
The industry you are employed in or provide services to; consumer goods, maritime, defence, telecommunication, financial services and education management, etc. You can also include industries that you worked in inprevious jobs.

Make notes about the businesses you work for now and in the past: particular services they provide, type of customers you work with (internal/external), who those customers are, where they are based, the organisational structure (privately owned, SME, FTSE 100), anything special or different about the businesses you are in?

How do you work, what hours, who do you report to, where are you based, who do you work with. What type of people report to you? Who do you work with best? How do you like to report to people? What management or leadership suits you best? When have you been most productive and happiest? Where was that and why? Make a note of any patterns emerging.

How do you describe the organisation you work in? For example, if you work in the Corporate Social Responsibility department of a bank, you can be creative about this according to what you want to do next. You can place yourself firmly in financial services, or you can decide your sector is charity, or you can align yourself with the sectors you invest in: environmental sciences and medical devices etc. It's a way of getting out of what you do now and transitioning into something different.

Column Three: Knowledge and Networks
What and who do you know? This is partly as a consequence of columns one and two, but includes more personal elements. We often ignore the obvious – who we are and where have we come from - such as your life stage and culture. If you're a middle-aged, middle-class, Anglo-Irish working mother like me, there's no point trying to pretend you're not. There are some clients, for example who will relate to me, others that won't. I know who to target.

Sometimes your character traits can lead you into career directions. Add these to your list too. I am a speaker on confidence and this came about because I was a terribly shy child. I had to teach myself techniques to mask my social awkwardness and I moved into sales jobs because salespeople, like actors, are performing roles. I became great at listening to other people talk about their problems because I hated talking about myself. I was a great observer of people and their success and I started to train as a counsellor, then a coach and this is how the material for *Mind Flip* has come about.

1

Here is a list to spark some ideas. You may have already thought of some of these when you described your job function and sector.

- Languages
- Family background
- Cultural origin, age, gender
- Personality traits and character
- Peer group characteristics
- Regulations/compliance you know about
- Systems, software, hardware
- Processes
- Projects you have worked on
- Education, qualifications, research interests
- Voluntary experience
- Passions and outside interests (in later life, people may come back to doing what they did most when they were younger, or incorporate this somehow)
- Networks; everyone you know, perhaps even your partner's or parents' network too
- Trends, changes and processes within your industry that can be relevant elsewhere and lessons learnt.
- What do you care about most at work?

By completing these three columns you can unlock patterns and clues to your expertise. The holy grail of career coaching is finding transferable skills: a way of transitioning into something different. If we stick with the Tarzan analogy, of each step leading to the next, you are picking up something from each job and by marketing it cleverly it gives you a step to the next job. You gradually get further away from where you started, by building on your skills, knowledge and networks all the time.

Do not underestimate the value of your network to a potential employer or user of your services. You aren't just hired because of your skillset. A crucial element of why you are valuable is who you know and how they can make you more productive immediately. This is why it can be hard to break into a new business area: you might have the skills on paper to do the job but you don't have the contacts, the go-to people and the established trust that makes life so much easier.

When I sold my recruiting recruiters business, I was approached by a company who sold recruitment software and wanted me to sell it to my contacts. Thanks, but no thanks. It's not only sales people who do this, to some extent it works for everyone: we all need trusted contacts on speed-dial so we can hit the ground running. Visual merchandisers need mannequin manufacturers or the best freelance window dressers; model agencies need bookers with their eye on the models of the future; account managers need prior knowledge of target accounts and so on. I read about a farmer who was hired by a soup company who knew other farmers who wanted to sell misshapen vegetables, which the supermarkets had rejected. Librarians understand the reading and logging in behaviours of particular groups of people. They know the firms who want to partner business with libraries, such as coffee shops and theatre companies trying to hire space. They might know management in the local authority and all the freelancers putting cards up on their noticeboards. They know the schools who visit and the publishing companies. Who is this network and information useful to? It all depends on what the librarian wants to do next but this is how you tap into the mysterious hidden job market; building on your network to create opportunities.

And it helps if you can bring more employees with you. Growing businesses like to hire new talent who can bring their previous colleagues with them, once their restrictive covenants have expired. These internal referrals are more likely to succeed than third party or external hires because they have already proved they can fit in.

Who wants you because of who you know? The answer is often right under your nose. It might be a direct competitor. It can also be someone who wants to do business with your contacts, or with your suppliers, or your previous contacts or previous employer. This is how people move sectors: they take their network and knowledge to another industry.

Your unique skillset
Take another piece of A4 paper and answer these questions.
- What is your brand?
- What is the perception you want people to have of you?
- What skills, expertise, knowledge and networks do you have?

Next make notes about how you can reinforce these. For example, are there networks you should be part of, professional associations you should be a member of, courses you need to take to become fully qualified, online articles you should write, or debates you could contribute to? Is this a big reinvention, or a natural evolution from where you are now? What support do you need to do this?

Combining all this information will help you target your job search. And most importantly: it will help tell you whose problems you can solve. And how can you make someone money or save them money by being on the payroll?

Exercise: My Skillset

Fill in the blanks below about you.

- This is what I do best and the skills and knowledge I enjoy using most.
- This is who I do it for.
- This is what keeps them awake at night.
- This is what they get out of working with me.
- This is why it matters to me.
- As a consequence of all this information, this is the type of organisation and the people I am targeting

Now you have to build up evidence for what you do, so you don't have to sell yourself anymore. You can sell the solution you offer to your targets' problems. You are selling your value.

How do you get your work to work for you?

There are three criteria that work needs to meet to be fulfilling.

1. Challenge

There needs to be sufficient challenge to absorb you in what you do. It's not realistic to expect your work to be like this all the time, but there must be some element of challenge. When were you last in flow, when you lost track of time? I had a client who said her work had become so dull that at lunchtimes she forgot about work, not the other way round.

2. Control

You need to be in control of your workload. This is the freedom to choose one task over another and some element of control over your working day/week/routine. The Whitehall Study into stress of civil servants (http://www.ucl.ac.uk/whitehall/) showed that stress was more prevalent at junior levels when people weren't in control of their workload. Senior people were less stressed because they were in control.

3. Commitment

This means having a sense of meaning from what you do. Are your values aligned with your work, do you feel like it matters? We covered this in The Soapbox Exercise in Chapter Three: *Be Marmite, not Vanilla.* Why do you go to work?

If one of these factors is missing, your work may not be fulfilling enough. Understanding which one might be missing for you helps you to make a decision as to whether you need to do something drastically different or make small adjustments.

PART
2

CRACK ON

This chapter will reveal how to unpack what you do and turn your case from hearsay to evidence. You've got it now. Recruiters don't want to read your subjective interpretation of your character traits. Nor do they want to read a list of your role responsibilities. They want to read quantifiable evidence of what you have achieved.

The best indicator of what a candidate will do in the future is what they have done in the past.

CHAPTER 6

Me, I'm brilliant

Now you need to work out what your achievements are and how you provide evidence of them.

What do you do, if you can't think of any achievements?

It's not uncommon to go blank at this, especially if you are in jobs with few definable outputs or performance measures. A good place to start is when you were happiest at work. Often we are happiest when we do what we are best at.

When were you happiest, most engaged, most engrossed in your work?

To answer this question, think about what you actually do/did at work; perhaps over the course of a month or whatever is an appropriate period of time to reflect the cycle of your work. If you feel you are plateauing in your role, go back further, when you were on a faster rising curve and felt motivated.

Make a note of what you actually did, breaking it down into tasks or actions. For example, you learnt how to use SAGE, typed minutes, managed junior sales people, pitched for new business, rewrote the Fire Practice procedure, took the morning register, fed the chickens, etc.

Be as specific as possible.
- What were you actually doing/achieving?
- What was the environment like?
- Who were you working with?
- What skills were you using?
- What was your brief?
- How were you being managed or led?
- What was the context?

Reflect on why you were you happy or unhappy then? Was it because of the task, or the team or context you were working in? What could be done to improve this picture? Make as many notes/mind maps as possible. It might also be helpful to think about what didn't get done when you were away from your workplace? Can you think of any feedback you received and what colleagues/customers/suppliers/management said about your skills.

If you want to be really scientific about it, write them into this grid below.

List the tasks against your skill level and rate how much enjoyment you got.

Enjoyable Skills Matrix

1. High Enjoyment, Low Skill	3. High Enjoyment, High Skill
2. Low Enjoyment, High Skill	4. Low Enjoyment, Low Skill

2

What does this tell you?

Are there tasks you enjoy doing but need to upskill (1)? Or parts of your work you are good at, but don't enjoy so much, so perhaps should start to leave them behind as you progress (2)? What should you lose all together (4)? It may be, you would enjoy using these skills more if you are better at them, or are you wasting time trying to develop non-core areas? Box 3 is the key to your expertise and therefore, the tasks that should appear most in any job description that interests you. Be aware of the next role you aspire to. Does your matrix reflect the skills you have now, or the skills you need to develop as you move upwards?

Here is an example, of a completed matrix of a Business Development Director.

1. High Enjoyment, Low Skill	3. High Enjoyment, High Skill
Pricing strategy, social media strategy, International sales New product development Managing non sales functions in the business like HR and finance	Strategic business reviews New business development Relationship management Client engagement Enterprise sales management Sales pitches Training rookies Recruiting sales teams
2. Low Enjoyment, High Skill	4. Low Enjoyment, Low Skill
Project Management Managing the marketing department Managing under performers Personal administration	Bid management Purchasing new CRM systems

This grid demonstrates that our Business Development Director, let's call him Jack, is in the right job. He's both skilled at and enjoys the core areas you'd expect from someone in his role. The areas he enjoys, but needs to get more experience at, could indicate where he could look for a new role. One that involves international markets and thinking creatively to develop new products and perhaps with more use of social media. Like many people in his role, he doesn't particularly enjoy the hassle of sales management (staff appraisal, managing underperformers), but is good at it. He is both unskilled and doesn't enjoy marketing strategy or PR, which indicates that he would be better working in a larger organisation with separate departments to do these (and he says he is good at collaboration) or where these roles are outsourced. Jack thinks he is weak at project management, so he needs to decide whether he needs training to progress, or if he needs to concentrate on his core business development skills.

Now, he needs to take what he thinks he is highly skilled at and get evidence for this that he can describe confidently, at interview and put into his CV.

Build your case of evidence

Recruiters don't want to know only what you do in your job. They want to know what you do over and above your job description.

- What's the purpose of your role and how do you know you are good at it?
- What is the legacy you will leave?
- What is the difference between an excellent and an average performer and how do you rate them? On that basis where do you fit?
- What do people say about you, when you aren't in the room?
- What's been your feedback at appraisals and on the job?
- What doesn't get done when you aren't in the business?
- How are you better or different from your peers?
- What did the job/business/team/clients/accounts etc. look like when you started the job and what does it look like now? This from – to should be how you describe each job on your CV.
- How did you perform against target or key performance indicators and where do you stand against your colleagues'/peers' performance?
- When did people thank you for a job well done?

2

- Any other quantitative measures: such as profits, revenues, return on investment, employee ratings, new sales numbers, product to market time, employee retention figures, employee satisfaction figures, margin, system efficiencies, market share?

You may be mucking out stables all your life, but you could do it quicker, safer and more cheerfully than anyone else and have a collection of thank you cards to prove it. You could understand the motivation of the particular people who come to those stables and have built a network with them, or you could have specific knowledge of the animals in those stables, or how to build stables, or how to make stables resilient in thunderstorms, or how to use waste in an environmentally friendly way. What can you do with this knowledge? Who needs it? You can always find these hooks to move forward into a new or different role.

I or we?

You may want to get input on this point from your past or present colleagues or managers: anyone who can remind you of what you have achieved. It might be team performance as well as your own; but think about what your contribution was to that result so you can talk about that, even if it was other people doing all the work to achieve the vision you set for them. It is still your leadership skill in defining the goal and creating the right environment and skilled team that enabled it to happen.

Now you have the facts, you can build them into a business case to show how good you are, without descending into the toe-curling clichés we are trying to avoid.

Avoid: *'I'm an extroverted tour guide who is passionate about customer services and really goes the extra mile.'*

Say: *'When I volunteered as a guide at the museum, I ensured that all the visitors had the best possible experience. I did this by making my talks as entertaining as possible, taking care of* *visitors with special needs, asking everyone in advance if there was anything they particularly wanted to learn about and being sensitive to the age and interests of each group. As a result my feedback scores from tour groups were never less than 85% when the average was 73%.'*

Now you have discovered what you have actually achieved in your career, you can put them into your CV and prepare to describe them at interview.

Examples of CV achievement statements

I grew the business from £1 million turnover to more than £3 million turnover, by increasing training on customer service and increasing sales focus within my teams. I created a VIP programme, targeting high net-worth London based professional males, mostly aged 35 – 55, which accounted for 13% of sales. I over-achieved on forecast by between 5% and 7% each year, which won me the Store Manager of the Year Award in 2016.

Although buying wasn't directly under my remit, I identified new designers who appealed to our customer base; introducing these new lines contributed to more than 22% of our profits.

I identified, devised and executed multi-channel online and offline B2B and B2C sales resulting in a 150% growth in commercial revenue during my tenure, including a 42% increase in revenue during the last two years.

I completed an 18-month secondment to the Department for Transport's Commercial team, which gave me an enhanced understanding of public sector procurement strategies. It also gave me an enhanced network of senior public sector decision-makers.

2

I project managed our office move from Hammersmith to Shoreditch, which I did on time and on budget (£27,500), with no reduction in consultant productivity.

A before and after CV

The first only lists role responsibilities.

- *I ran after school and holiday theatre workshops.*
- *I took bookings, arranged teachers, sent out communication to the parents and managed the bank account.*
- *I successful organised end of year performances, enjoyed by students and their parents.*

The second shows achievements in a much more narrative style, which builds a real picture of what happened.

- *When I took over the theatre school it was making a loss of about £2000 a term and had only 37 students. By the end of the second year, it was making an average profit of more than £26,500 per term, despite using an extra six teachers and more space. Currently we have 200 students and there is always a waiting list.*

The most popular way of describing your achievements at Interview

Now you take those bullet points and expand them into interview answers. You explain what you have done without pointing out how brilliant they are. The results speak for themselves and your brilliance. In a competency based interview you are asked for examples. For example, describe a time when..., tell me about how you have... etc... but you should be prepared for these examples for any kind of formal or informal meeting. The trick is to prepare at least three or four great examples of how you have already solved their problems. Interesting examples of what you want them to know and you make sure you get the message across. Trying to drum up examples for each competency on the job description doesn't always hammer the point home that you have already fulfilled the role responsibility successfully. When you are talking about what you have done, rather than you as a person, you stop thinking about yourself and your confidence and passion builds.

The most popular format for describing achievements is STAR.

Situation - what the problem/issue was
Task - what needed to be done and why
Action - what you actually did about it
Result - the results/outcomes you got

Some people use CAR as a tidier method.

Context - describing the problems/issues involved
Action - what you did to solve them
Result - results/outcome

In either case, the results section is particularly important. HR Managers like to understand what you have achieved and lessons you have learnt and perhaps, if relevant, what you would do differently if faced with the same problem again. If you are a manager, it's great to add how you have used the learning from this experience to develop your team. For example: *'Next time we had this situation, we dealt with it more quickly at the planning stage before it escalated into a supply chain issue.'*

Example of an evidence based interview answer

Question: What's your view on managing underperformers?

Avoid: I'm quite strong on this actually. I like to make people fully aware of my expectations, manage their performance actively and make them immediately aware when they are falling short.

Say: *Let me give you an example of someone who was underperforming in my team when I took over the role last April. One of the Account Managers had been consistently falling short on target and my predecessor had started a performance management programme with them the month before.*

(S) *This was a crucial role in the team and so I decided to really focus on this one individual. I wasn't sure if they didn't have the skills for the job, were lacking in motivation or what the issue was and neither was the HR Manager. I needed to know this, as well as ensuring they knew exactly what was expected of them.*

(T) *I met with this individual weekly for a formal 1:1 as well as going out on client meetings with them to watch them at work. I noticed they were strong on relationship management and very organised with their paperwork and administration. The problem seemed to be they were reluctant to actually ask for the business. On careful questioning, it turned out that it was the closing skills, which were missing.*

(A) *We talked about this, I put them on a training course and got them mentoring within the business from one of the more senior account managers. This helped develop the senior account manager as well as building team relationships, so it was a win-win situation.*

(R) *The result was their performance improved and they are now over achieving on target. I decided to do a skills analysis of the rest of the team to plug any other skills gaps.*

As well as nailing the question you are asked, your answer covers a number of other competencies (such as; leadership, people management, assessing training needs, performance managing, building teams, coaching skills and so on). At no stage do you have to point out what a great manager you are, how good your communication skills are, how your team love you or any other opinion. You are keeping to the facts. Bingo.

People think in pictures not words.
Drawing a visual picture in your interview answers
means they will understand what you do and the
value you can bring to them.

It can feel quite laborious going into this level of detail, but this is how you score well in interviews nowadays. It's the system. It means that the candidate who gets the job is the one who is best at the system, as opposed to actually doing the job. That's why many external hires don't work and why yet again, employers would rather offer the job to an internal candidate because they know what they are getting.

Candidates for internal promotions can trip up when they are on a competency based interview of course, particularly talking about what they do for people who know them. You know what I do so why I am talking all this blarney? In theory because of course, interviewees are biased whether they realise it or not you are only as good as your performance at interview. You have to answer like this to get the top scores. At least you are talking factually with a case behind you which makes you feel proud of what you do. Even if you want to say; *'Look you know I can do the job, so give it to me and let's all get back to work.'*

2

This chapter will help you to ensure you get yourself into the right mind set before interviews and show you the tricks to ensuring brilliant competency based interviews, every time. Also, we will explore the good, unusual and annoying questions, as well as those that they should never ask you.

Don't think of where you are now in your life.
Think about where you are planning to be.
Look and behave like you are there already.
How would you perform if you knew you were
going to get offered the job?
Behave like that now.

CHAPTER 7

The Interview Minefield

Mind Flipping is all about selling yourself based on the value of what you do and the solution you provide. Although you don't want to be self-deprecating or shy on describing your achievements because both are counterproductive. You are only as good as your answers and you can't expect the interviewers to fill in the gaps. You have to tell them how great you will be for them based on what you have done in the past.

The chances are that if you are having a formal interview in a largish organisation it will be a competency-based interview. Together with a work sample to see you actually performing in the role, a competency-based interview is proven to have far more validity as a selection tool than the traditional biographical interview.

Competency-based interview
This is when two or more people are interviewing you and the questions are pre-set. Each candidate is asked the

same questions and the better your answers the better you score and the top scoring candidate gets the job offer. The process is supposed to remove bias. Of course, subconscious bias still exists, but you can work this to your advantage by demonstrating excellent interpersonal skills and emotional intelligence throughout.

'Competencies are the specific behaviour patterns (including knowledge, skills and abilities a job holder is required to demonstrate in order to perform the relevant job tasks with competence.'

John Arnold, 2003

The purpose of a competency-based interview is to gain an understanding of how you have dealt with specific situations in past roles. This is evidence of what you are likely to do in your next one. The best indicator of how successful a candidate will be in the future is of course, how they have performed in the past.

One of my clients described this process as; *'walking a tightrope over alligators.'* I do love an animal metaphor! However, it doesn't have to be like that if you anticipate the questions and prepare properly. Ask yourself, if you were the interviewer what information would you want to know to prove that the candidate could hit the ground running in the role? What questions would you ask to find that information?

It's a good idea to prepare for all interviews - as well as researching the company and their background and future prospects - as if they were competency based. Use the STAR format from the previous chapter. People think in more pictures not words and your answers need to paint those visual case studies.

To help you practice here are four sample competencies and questions that could be asked to assess them. You'll see that some of the questions can cover more than one competency - as we discussed in the STAR/CAR section – so give great case studies that cross several competencies at once. Expect to be asked more technical questions also. A good result is when the interviewers run out of questions to ask. It usually means you have covered all the competencies.

Problem solving and decision-making

Here what they are looking for includes your demonstrated ability to:
- take ownership of problems and decisions;
- empower other people to problem solve and make decisions; and
- step in to long running problems and hold the right people accountable for solving them.

Example questions
- What's your problem solving style?
- Do you manage your activities to minimise or avoid them?
- Describe a time when you were able to get people working together effectively in a challenging situation and what the outcome was.
- Tell me about a difficult decision you had to make.
- Have you experienced a situation that was slipping out of control?
- What did you do about it?

Capability building

Here what they are looking for includes your demonstrated ability to:
- Manage the performance of your team and developing the skills and behaviours needed within the team in order to meet the organisation's objectives;
- Adapt your leadership style to get best performance from individual team members;

- Put in succession plans;
- Look at learning and developing plans from an ROI perspective;
- Improve skillsets through stretch assignments; and
- Provide feedback to improve performance.

Example questions
- Describe a time when you have had to get buy-in from all members of a team.
- Explain a time when you served as a mentor to someone outside your own team and what the outcomes were.
- Explain a strategy for employee improvement.
- Describe a situation when you had to deliver negative feedback and how you handled it.
- Have you had any subordinates with performance problems? What have you done about them?

Partnership and communication
Here what they are looking for includes your demonstrated ability to:
- act as a team for the good of the organisation as a whole;
- work cross-functional and effectively to get the job done; and
- build collaborative relationships with internal and external customers and partners.

Example questions
- Describe a time when you had to use your communication skill in a difficult situation.
- Describe an achievement that required you to work with a diverse team.
- How do you resolve conflict in the team you are part of?
- How have you executed a plan of consistent communication to everyone involved in a project?
- What types of upward communication systems have you established?

- How often do you attend meetings with your peers and what role do you play in them?

Customer focus

Here what they are looking for includes your demonstrated ability to:

- put customers at the heart of all work;
- get clear information on customers and use it to ensure expectations are met or exceeded;
- create and maintain customer relationships; and
- consider internal and external customers.

Example questions

- Explain a time when you have repaired a damaged customer relationship and what the outcome was.
- Describe a scenario when a customer's needs took priority above yours and the companys.
- Explain a strategy for exceeding expectations within your customer base.
- How do you handle negative customer feedback?

Respect the silences

I've interviewed candidates who have given great answers but then continued to talk and talk, undoing all the good impression they had made. Know when to shut up! Interviews are the same as any other any social interaction. Communicate as naturally as possible. Talking over people, or not picking up clues to stop talking, won't get you hired. Pause and draw breath, allow the interviewers to make notes, to think and to formulate their next question. Make your point and draw breath, while the penny drops about your brilliance. You can always ask; *'Would you like more detail on that'* if you feel you have more of value to add. A brain dump of everything you know about the topic is rarely what is required and anyway, you will be told if that's the case.

I remember letting a couple of candidates rabbit on when I was an interviewer. They wouldn't stop and I decided that there was no way I was going to do anything with them. I thought - if they were rude enough to give me a lengthy monologue - I was going to switch off and think about something else. Or in one case, update my to-do list, which fortunately I had with me. The interviewees, in their arrogance, never noticed my inattention. They had a great time, hearing their own voice. In actual fact, interviewers who get to ask great questions and enjoy hearing their voices, give candidates much higher ratings.

How they really score you

They might feel like alligators as you walk the tightrope, but interviewers are subject to normal human subconscious bias and vulnerabilities like everyone else. How competency based interviews works in the real world is that when you leave the interview room, the other panelists look to the Chair of the Panel and say; 'What did you think about Tony?' The Chair says; *'I thought he was excellent, particularly on Governance and Strategy'* and the others, keen to look like they are as clever as the Chair, all nod in agreement and score accordingly. HR professionals, well trained in interview skills, might score as they go and stick to their scores. Other panel members, mere mortals, listen to your answer, make notes and score when you leave because they don't want you to spot the numbers on their pad. The human factor is so important. You can give textbook answers, but if they think they can't work with you they will drop your scores.

Tricky interview questions

As well as the standard competency and technical questions for your role, which you can anticipate and your case studies, which you will have prepared, also think about some other patterns of questioning. I keep a huge file of clever or unusual or downright annoying questions, which my clients have been asked over years and here's a selection of each to help you.

Clever questions

- Which bosses have you worked for who got the best out of you and why?
- Conversely, which managers have you had least respect for and why?
- Which company's culture fitted you best?
- What are your colleagues saying about you now when you are out of the room?
- What do you do differently from your peers?
- What was your journey like to get where you are?
- How do you want to be remembered?
- How do you learn?
- How do you manage failure?
- What's the biggest mistake you have ever made?
- Describe your worst day and your best day.

Unusual questions

- What are you really into outside of work?
- Put in rank order, which is most important to you: vision; execution; and collaboration.
- What do you struggle most with at work?
- Define a moral dilemma and tell me when you have faced one and what the outcome was.
- Tell me why I shouldn't outsource your job.
- You have a consulting background and I hate consultants. Why should I hire you?
- Explain derivatives to me as if I was your Granny.
- You're good. What question can't you answer?
- What don't you want me to ask you today?
- What's your blind spot?
- What's your greatest fear?

2

Annoying questions
- How many table tennis balls are there in China?
- How many manhole covers are there in New York City?
- How many people in the world share your birthday?
- What kind of animal would you be?
- If you were a dog, what breed would you be?

The clever questions make you think and help the Interviewer to really understand you. They are increasingly common, particularly the ones about learning from failure (building resilience). The unusual ones are great questions that are used less frequently. It's hard to anticipate every question like this but if you are clear on the message you want to get across about your skillset and career goals you should be fine. None of these should be bear traps - it is as much how you answer the question and all your interpersonal skills - as it is the answer itself. You can't practice for every question and it's probably good that you don't; or you will look too contrived. Learning to improvise and stay on message is a good skill. You can always say; *'that's a great question, I've never been asked before, right – let me think....'*

The downright annoying questions were used to test graduates on their problem solving styles and their ability to cope under pressure. It's much more effective to put the candidate under pressure than to ask hypothetically, how they cope with it. The dog question was a favourite of an IT recruiter who was unencumbered by political correctness. He is no longer in the recruitment industry.

Questions they should never ask you
Candidates should only be questioned about their ability to do the job. Your personal life, age, sexuality or ethnic background, are irrelevant. The exception to these guidelines is when there is an occupational requirement for a role and the employer can objectively justify why a certain type of candidate is required.

For example, a religious organization may stipulate that only candidates of that religion should apply, if it is a genuine requirement of the role.

It is legal to ask about ethnic background on application forms but this is for monitoring purposes only and usually anonymous. It should not be brought up at interview, although asking you about the languages you speak is of course, a good thing. By law they have to check you are eligible to work in the UK, but there is no obligation that English needs to be your mother tongue. You could say; *'I am fully eligible to work in the UK and speak and write English fluently. As you can see I got a 2:1 in my degree.'*

2

You can be asked about your religious practices only if this is about work scheduling, such as; *'Can you work in the days required for the role?'* It is not legal to ask you about your beliefs, such as; *'Which religious holidays do you observe?'*

Generally, a trained interviewer will stick to your suitability to doing the job, your commitment and motivation and your career goals. Even asking you questions, such as where you live can cause issues if it is in an area heavily populated by a specific ethnic group or social class. They should stick to specifics, such as; *'Are you able to start work at 8 am?'*

There is no obligation upon you to disclose criminal convictions provided your sentence is already spent. An employer should not refuse employment because of a previous crime, unless it relates to the role in question, such as working as a teacher or handling money for example. Criminal record checks are carried out for some roles by the Disclosure and Barring Service (DBS). They can ask you if there are any reasons why you may not legally be able to take up the position.

Interviewers without training may ask you questions that make you feel uncomfortable. The trick is to go with the flow and use humour; 'I'm not sure why it is relevant if I am married, why do you think it is?' If they keep pushing and you feel really uncomfortable, you can say you prefer not to answer because you keep your personal and professional life separate. However, you are keen to find more out about the role, so you'd rather talk more about that. Or, you can say, you don't think this is the right environment for you and leave. It's your choice.

Look like you fit in

Part of fitting in is cultural fit and for this reason; be judicious about disclosing your beliefs and views. You can't be asked about political affiliations or group memberships, unless they are relevant to the role. Avoid mentioning them unless you are sure they are a point in your favour. They can't reduce your interview scores if you are an active union representative for example, but if you are in an interview with an organization that doesn't encourage union membership, then they will subconsciously file you under; 'not like us' and that will have a *'horns effect'* - when you score badly across all competencies - the opposite of a halo effect.

Of course, interviews are a two way process. If you are passionate about fox hunting, you might not want to work with a team of hunt saboteurs, for example. It is best to find out now.

There is more about biased questioning in Chapter 16: *Returners, Mums and Carers; Never Mind the Gap*

The Long Train Journey Test
One of my clients tested for these four factors when interviewing.

- Technical ability: can they do the job well?
- Ambition: how badly do they want to do the job?
- Commitment: do they want to work with us?
- Do we like them: do we want to go on a long train journey with them?
  (David Schwartz, *The Magic of Thinking Big* calls 'likeability')

Once the interview process is over and you are offered the job, remember you will be working with these people. If the CEO is hiring you as an interim to do an unpopular change process for example, then possibly she/he might not care if they like you or not. However, for most of us the team we work with is one of our main reasons for going to work so your 'likeability factor will play a big part in them choosing you over the other candidates. They are going to be stuck with you!

People who get to the very top have lofty ambitions matched with great interpersonal skills. I have seen people succeed when their ambition and emotional intelligence exceed their intellectual ability - but they are usually smart enough to surround themselves with a great team. How genuinely likeable you are is critically important in job interviews. It won't mitigate against poor preparation of course, but organisations look for the best cultural fit. Do we like them and are they one of us?

We usually like people when we feel liked by them. We think they like us because they show an interest in us, which makes us feel special. Here's a way to be more likeable during the selection process.

Zena's Likeability Formula

- **Remember the interviewers names.** It sounds obvious but I have met people who have been on interviews and can't follow up because they don't know the names of the people they were introduced to. Ask their name and pronounce it the way they pronounce it. Write it down and send them a thank you email or LinkedIn invitation. It is time consuming to meet prospective candidates, be respectful and acknowledge that.

- **Show an interest in the interviewer.** Leave your ego at the door. Massage the interviewer's ego instead. Ask them about their own careers, time in the organization, opinion about the main challenges of the role etc. You are an expert at what you do, but you don't know it all and want their input. This isn't just a likeability tactic either; you'll learn much about the role from listening to them.

- **Be sincere.** You are being your best self here – what John Lees, *How to Find a Job you'll Love*, calls you on your best day – but be yourself. That's the person you are going to be when you start work after all.

- **Be as relaxed as possible.** Of course, you will be on edge and that's a good thing. But you want to project an air of professional competence. *'Nothing phases me. Dump all your problems on me and I will fix them for you. I will relieve your stress, not add to it.'*

- **Smile when you meet them.** I was a very shy child and learnt that putting a smile on my face was a great strategy for hiding my social anxieties. Smiling on the outside makes you feel more positive and relaxed on the inside. Try it!

- **Have a confident handshake and make eye contact.** You may think that's obvious, but here's a test. Sit in a business's reception area and watch people coming to meet their visitors. Check who actually makes proper eye contact – not just a glance at the person - but actually looking at them in the eye. Not many. Taking a second to do this deliberately says you are interested in the other person and want to get to know them.

- **Praise them on their successes.** Tell them why you are interested in working there. We all feel vulnerable. Employers like to get external feedback on how they compare to other companies. You can say things such as; *'you are the first organization that has mentioned to me about X'* or *'that's a great question I haven't been asked that before.'* Never be indiscrete, but genuine positive feedback goes a long way.

The worse it feels, the better it's going

Contrary to how it might feel, it is usually a good sign if an Interviewer appears to be giving you a tough time. Generally, they probe more when they like you and want to drill down into your experience. When I was a recruiter my heart would sink when a candidate rang to say how nice the interviewer had been to them. It usually meant they hadn't thought it was worth their time to really push the candidate and the answer was going to be a No.

If the job involves working under pressure, they shouldn't say; *'How do you cope with pressure?'* to explore this. They usually make you demonstrate it by asking difficult questions and seeing how you cope. That can be why you are asked direct questions to see if you can push back a little, such as; *'Why did you leave within the first year'* or *'I bet you regret making that decision?'*

Help yourself by preparing thoroughly: it can take a day or two to do this properly. As well as understanding the business problem you can solve, you need to know everything about the company: financials; PR; their employer brand; how they interact on social media; and what their customers say about them, etc. Learning the home page of their website won't cut it. Make notes and take them with you. You wouldn't go into a business meeting without notes. This isn't Dragons Den. Take a smart file with you with notes and questions you want to ask and look like you are working in the role already.

Golden Rules
- **Never under estimate your own ability:** spell out what you have achieved.
- **Never over estimate the interviewer:** avoid jargon they don't understand and never assume they have read your CV and know all your achievements and that they aren't as nervous as you.

The biggest trap of all
Never criticise your last employer; no matter how justified you feel. Interviewers assume you will repeat all your behaviour patterns in their organisation. If you blame other people for what's gone wrong in your last role; they think you will blame them when things go wrong with them. Always acknowledge what went well - perhaps hinting at the problems - coupled with a positive reason for moving on. Here are a few examples to help you.

'My line manager was excellent at the technical side of the job, however for advice on managing my team I always went to a couple of the more experienced managers who were really supportive. They have now left the business and I don't feel I am getting the management development I need at this stage of my career. I am keen to find a business with a reputation for great leadership so when I read the article about your award.'

'It's a shame the redundancy programme has happened because a couple of years ago it was such an ambitious organisation with really inspirational growth plans. I've learnt so much there and I want to find another business with the energy that we had when I was happiest there.'

'The senior leadership team who were the reason for me joining the firm have all left and although my performance is still on budget I don't have the same relationship with their successors. I can't see a long term future but it's taught me so much about working in a professional partnership and navigating internal politics.'

2

Never make excuses for obvious mistakes if they raise them. You aren't expected to be perfect. You need to be coachable though, with a desire to learn from your mistakes and always improve your performance. How skilfully you handle the skeleton in the closet – the question you don't want to be asked – can be the reason why you get offered the job. Show your emotional intelligence, ambition and commercial savvy. Tell them what you regret doing and what you would do differently next time. Bring it up yourself if they are skirting around it: they might not know how to ask the question. If you have been made redundant; tell them if you need to and be as honest as you can, as per the example below.

'To be honest, I was shocked when I was told I had been selected for redundancy. There hadn't been any performance issues with my work – in fact, I was promoted three times in five years - and it never occurred to me; I would be the one in the team who had to go. I think my mistake was spending too much time on existing accounts and not enough on developing new ones. I had junior account managers who can continue to work with the major accounts I had developed and the business will be more profitable without my salary. I really enjoy new business development so will make sure I keep doing an element of this next time, even if it's not my focus.'

Often people haven't achieved much in the months leading up to redundancy and it may be that you need to explain it.

'This was the second redundancy programme in three years. I knew I would be able to take voluntary redundancy and although I have wanted to leave for a while, I have hung on as I wanted to put my hand up and benefit from the generous package on offer. I have been there for a long time and it's great to have been able to take off a chunk of the mortgage. I have been doing contract work more or less since I've left and that's given me real insight into how other organisation run these projects and of course into other work cultures. I am keen to work here because I like the way you....'

All these explanations have a sense of energy and momentum. You aren't dwelling on the past; but moving forward with what you want to do next.

Never hold back your enthusiasm.
They want to see that you are motivated to work for them.
Go into the room with the intention of getting a job offer.
The only game you should play is your 'A' Game –
your very best self.

Presentations

These are a fairly standard part of most selection processes now and are often more about your ability to summarise, think strategically, present and hold your nerves, rather than your technical ability or getting the answers exactly right.

As an interviewer who has witnessed these go badly, here are some real basics.

- Stick to the time slot. Four minutes means four minutes.
- If they ask you to present on 'three strategic options' call your presentation 'three strategic options', not 'the way forward' or any other interpretations. Zero points for not following instructions.
- Avoid power point unless specifically asked to use it.
- Prepare a really impressive handout with a more detailed strategy than in your four-minute or otherwise brief presentation. Give it to them at the beginning so they can make notes as you talk.

2

This chapter will help you understand how psychometric tests measure your cognitive ability and personality traits so you can face them with more confidence.

CHAPTER 8

Psychometric tests: How do you tick?

The so-called 'father of vocational guidance' was a former engineer, lawyer and school teacher in Boston called Frank Parsons. In 1908 he set up one of the world's first career-counselling services, using an elaborate system of assessing personality traits. Unfortunately he was an adherent of the now-defunct 'science' of phrenology and believed a person's character could be assessed by measuring their cranial depressions and prominences. Read Roman Krznaric's *How to Find Fulfilling Work* for more detail. Fortunately, work psychologists went on to develop series of questions, which proved to be a far more valid and reliable method of measuring our cognitive ability and personality dimensions than the bumps on our head.

Some form of psychometric assessment is now a common part of the selection process. These days they are usually conducted remotely online. Tests can be cognitive ability tests, which are 11 plus style verbal or numerical reasoning tests. These have right and wrong answers and are a straight forward pass or fail. Make sure you find a quiet place and time to complete the tests without interruptions from people or devices. You usually have practice questions before you start. Also, there are practice papers on the Internet. Search on 'practice aptitude tests'. Sometimes the questions come quickly after the test finishes – as soon as you press the button, obviously – and this has wrong-footed people. Usually these are best done early in the day, after a caffeine fix, but choose the time you feel most alert.

You may be asked to complete more fun personality tests, which help your potential employer understand how you behave at work. Strictly speaking the latter should not be used to fail you, but to give an idea of how to get the best performance out of you if they hire you. However, common sense dictates that they can flag up problems, such as low agreeableness or emotional stability, which can influence their decision.

As part of the test licence, the candidate should get feedback on their results, so ask if you don't. Most people enjoy reading about themselves. You may be offered a 1:1 session with an organisational psychologist or other trained assessor to give you feedback. Usually they find the test results to be spot on, if slightly exaggerated. Many of the tests compare the real you with how other people see you, which are called the situational results.

The Big Five major personality factors

1. **Extroversion** – warmth, gregariousness, assertiveness, activity, excitement seeking, positive emotions.
2. **Neuroticism** – anxiety, angry hostility, depression, self-consciousness, impulsiveness, vulnerability.
3. **Conscientiousness** – competence, order, dutifulness, achievement striving, self-discipline, deliberation.
4. **Agreeableness** – trust, straightforwardness, altruism, compliance, modesty, tender-mindedness.
5. **Openness to experience** – fantasy, aesthetic, feelings, action, ideas, values.
(Work Psychology, John Arnold, 2005)

How your personality is matched to the job

Tests need to be carefully planned and assessed to have significant incremental validity in a selection process, scrupulously matching the job requirements to the personality traits required; what they call the predictor and criterion variables. For example, not all of us need to show high levels of extroversion, unless we are in roles that need it, such as sales.

Huge amounts of research have been conducted on personality assessment with fascinating results. For example, conscientiousness correlates most highly with overall job performance, compared to the other Big Five personality dimensions but this is negatively correlated with creativity (a competency for many different job roles). In this situation, the individual facets of conscientiousness are differentially important. (Hough and Furnham, 2003). You can't screen out people who aren't highly conscientious because you might lose their rare creative talent. Another example is dependability, a facet of conscientiousness, which correlates 0.18 with overall job performance in sales jobs, but only 0.03 with overall job performance in managerial jobs. Openness to experience tends to be positively correlated with training performance across many job roles (Hough and Furnham, 2003). That's also why showing an appetite for change and learning is vital throughout the recruitment process.

You can see why these tests have to be set and assessed by highly trained experts. More work needs to be done on the impact of cultural differences in personality testing, particularly when personality assessment is being used on global recruitment campaigns (Arnold, 2005). As yet again, the 'norms' can be 'people like us' which can discriminate against the people who aren't. You could point out cross-cultural issues that might have a bearing on your test results, correlating them with the results you have achieved.

Common tests you might be asked to complete

NEO P-IR Personality Questionnaire
This takes about 25 minutes to complete and measures personality traits across five domains in relation to your behavioural preferences, both in and out of work.

The Hogan Development Survey (HDS)
This measures behavioural tendencies that influence an individual's leadership style and actions based on deeply ingrained personality traits. It identifies how, if natural strengths are overplayed, they might become weaknesses and impede work relationships or hinder productivity. It takes about 20 minutes.

The FIRO-B
This takes about 10 minutes and measures your interpersonal preferences in relation to your interactions with people.

The Myers-Briggs Type Indicator (MBTI)

A popular test base on the theory of Carl Jung, who speculated that there are four principal psychological functions by which humans experience the world: sensation; intuition; feeling; and thinking. And that one of these four functions is dominant for a person most of the time. It takes about 30 minutes to complete.

Get in the right frame of mind

Don't try to bluff your way through a psychometric test. It is vital that you don't try and fake your answers. The majority of tests include a scale to assess intentional distortion (Arnold, 2003) and warn you of the potential consequences of faking.

However, it is equally important that you get yourself into the right work mind set before you start answering the questions. For example, I learnt the hard way when one of my clients' who was totally chilled on garden leave, produced results which demonstrated a lack of motivation and dominance in her tests! Since then, I've made sure my clients spend a few minutes getting a work head on, casting their minds back to a time when they were succeeding at work and feeling at the top of their game. Remind yourself of the value you can bring to this organisation and the cast-iron achievements you have already notched up.

Stand up, stretch out and make your physical self more imposing if it helps. Another of my clients put his suit on to get into the right frame of mind. This is so important if you are feeling a bit vulnerable about your career situation. You don't want this temporary state of mind to come across as a fixed one, so do whatever you need to do – physically and mentally – to present your best self.

Milk the results

While it is tempting to be relieved that they haven't spotted all your neuroses and file the results away, you can use the feedback in several ways to help you.

A clever candidate will use them to anticipate competency-based questions they'll be asked on interview. Tests, such as the McQuaig Word Survey® suggest questions for the interviewer to probe deeper into how you manage your natural tendencies when they could get in the way of your performance or relationships with other people. For example, a candidate who shows a ruthless, hard driving, high achieving style could be asked; *'Tell me about a time when you had to stay positive to get a project completed, despite obstacles'* or *'Can you tell me about a time when you faced a number of setbacks in your job? How did you handle it and how did you maintain the morale of your team?'*

The words and phrases in the test results can be an enormously helpful resource, giving you new language to describe yourself on your CV, at interview and also in the on-boarding phase of a new role. It explains how you like to work. Of course, don't use them on their own in a bull 'change shaper and ideas generator' way but illustrated with quantitative measures as much as possible and demonstrating the value of what you can do for them. Here is an example.

'I thrive on driving change programmes, which is what I did at Trynder Inc to hit that £30m target. So if the role needs me to keep a firm hand on the tiller and manage existing business I'm probably not the right person for you. What I could do is help you move into new markets, for example the leisure and health sector which is where most of my revenue has come from this year. How does that fit with your strategy?'

They also help you become much more self-aware, which is really useful if you are considering a number of different career options. If your natural style is more entrepreneurial and independent than you are demonstrating at work for example, then self-employment could be a good option for you. If you are highly extroverted, then always working at home alone won't suit you and you will need to make a plan to re-energise with regular networking events, and conference calls or meet-ups.

Do your career goals reflect the findings of the psychometric or should you revaluate them?

2

This chapter busts the personal statement myths and demonstrates how to make a much more effective use of these to show your true value to your next employer. The personal statement or profile section is usually at the top of the CV, under your name and contact details. Generally, no one reads it because they are full of old rubbish and recruiters are none the wiser about what you do when they have ploughed their way through it.

CHAPTER 9

Personal statements: Who are you?

Think about when you have done any hiring in the past and what was your experience of personal statements? When I researched personal statements, 300 recruiters, employers and HR professionals - without exception and with varying degrees of rudeness – said they look at the most recent job on the CV first, to see if it relevant to them; then if it is, they skim the personal statement, rarely bothering to read it before checking out the rest of the document.

However, a really good statement can have a mitigating effect on a weaker CV.

For example, here is a real peach, sent to me by a frustrated recruiter.

'Marketing, sales and customer service experienced, MSc Marketing and communication degree, is seeking a challenging position to leverage personal knowhow and skills into sales and marketing, communication and *customer service field. Quick learner, able to grasp new ideas and concepts. Enjoys being part of a successful team. Results-driven, quality-focused with a keen eye for attention to detail coupled with the perseverance to seek effective solutions under time pressure. Educated, honest and reliable. Able to build and maintain efficient work relationships, patient and enthusiastic.*

A good personal statement includes:…
- a summary of your career to date;
- what you want to do next; and
- the skills or knowledge or experience that bridge the two.

Your value
The rest of the CV is evidence for what you put into the statement and shows the value of what you do, not your personality characteristics.

Here are several good examples.

'CIPD qualified HR professional with eight years' experience managing people, resource and service delivery within the NHS. Now looking to move to the private sector, specifically looking to use acquired knowledge of employment law and employee relations in an organisation wishing to improve their employment policies and procedures.'

'After many years performing all round the world as a successful ballet dancer, I am now enjoying a second career as a qualified well-being practitioner. I use my expertise of how the mind and body work in synchronicity to maximise the well-being of busy professionals and improve their work performance.'

This section does not have to be titled: Personal Statement. It can be more effective to title it: What I am looking for; followed by; What I have to offer; with bullet point showing specific skills, for example as below.

What I am looking for: I want to utilise my significant management accountancy experience, alongside my knowledge of donation management, by moving to a Finance Business Partner role within a larger charity.

What I have to offer:
- I am able to develop and implement best practices in donation management, and trust fund accounting; and
- detailed knowledge of Charity Commission requirements, particularly Charities and Reserves (CC19).

2

A recruiter can read these and immediately understand what you do best and the type of role you are looking for next. Stating what you want is important: the best candidates, the 'talent', tend to have clearer goals and be more assertive about what they are looking for.

The acid test is if a junior in the HR department can read your personal statement and understand what they are getting. *'We have a candidate here who is looking for a new challenge and is self-motivated and reliable'* isn't a compelling proposition. But *'I have a CV of a store manager selling high-end Swiss watches who has over-achieved his targets for the last five years and who wants to relocate to Dublin'* gives them something to work with. They may not have anything for them now, but at least they will remember him when they do and they will at least file him in the right place on their database.

Splice your personal statement into your opening gambit at interview.

The most important interview preparation you can do is to prepare your answer to the 'tell me about yourself' question. First impressions are crucial.

When you are asked; *'Tell me about yourself'* or whatever question is used at the beginning of the interview to explore your motivation for wanting the role, use the structure of the personal statement to frame your answer. This provides context to the entire interview and the rest of the interview reinforces these facts with the evidence for what you said at the start. It also quells nerves if you have a good opening gambit prepared. It's like learning poetry, if you remember the first couple of words, the rest will flow.

Anchor what you want to do smack bang into their problem. When interviewers ask the question what they are really saying is; *'Who are you again and what have you got for me and please don't waste my time.'* If you start with; *'Er well as you can see from my CV'* you've lost them already and it is hard to come back from that.

Here are several examples of what to say at the start of the interview to any of those; *'Why are you here'* questions.

'I have been an HR Director in the NHS for the last twelve years and I now want to take my understanding of best practices and regulation into the private sector, ideally an NHS supplier where my network and knowledge would be most useful. Obviously, I am really interested in Medi-Instruments because I feel you are at exactly at the right stage of growth to need someone like me.'

'I have been working in supply chain management in the consumer sector and had a really interesting roller-coaster ride with Red Jams Ltd across three continents. I feel that my FMCG experience is relevant to the pharmaceutical sector because it is experiencing some of the same global supply

chain issues we have solved in the past. I wanted to talk to you more about this and see if there are any synergies.'

'I've had a fantastic time selling paper with Writesmiths - they give such great training too - and developed a really strong client base across professional services businesses, including law firms and accountancy practices. I've decided that my next career move should be to sell a higher value product and I know my clients would love your water-coolers as much as I do. I wanted to find out more about the business and if you think I'd be the right fit for you.'

Answering like this puts you in control of the interview. You are setting the agenda, being business like, showing you know what you want and that you have thought through about their problems. It's about you and what you want, but factual and specific. Build on this strong first impression by using the case studies in the previous chapter and keep building on it throughout the process. This is the most important preparation you can do for interviews.

2

Exercise: Opening Gambit

- Tell us about you.
- Why are you interested in this job?
- What are you going to say?
- They don't want to know about your early childhood.
- They want to know what you do in a clear way to enable them to repeat it to their boss later.
- What you want to do next?
- How does this job dovetail with your career ambitions?

Walk the talk

How you behave provides evidence of how you behave at work. Prove that you have the skill and characteristics they ask for. If the job specification calls for a warm, outgoing personality, why not pick up the phone and ring the recruiter to chat with them about the vacancy, rather than emailing them. And remember to engage with the receptionist and anyone else you meet when you attend an interview. If they are asking for project management skills, ask questions about the next stage in the process. You can't say you are hard-working and then have a CV full of long breaks in between jobs. Or that you have great attention to detail and have spelling mistakes in your application letter. Passion and enthusiasm come across in the effort you put into your application, not because you have put them in a boring list of bullet points. If the job description says you have to be pro-active, make sure you call or email the interviewer to follow up. Send them something relevant that you mentioned during the interview, email them to thank them for their time, anything to build a relationship.

Coping with rejection if you don't get offered the job

Statistically, it is highly improbable you will get every single job offered to you, no matter how convincing you are. If they don't think you are right for them that could be a personality fit or that the role isn't right for you right now. Candidates can take rejection personally and make all kinds of assumptions, such as; *'They think I am too old, it's because I have been out of the market for too long, my experience isn't good enough'* etc. Those might be the right answers, but they wouldn't have called you in for an interview if you couldn't do the job on paper. Usually interviews are to assess fit and motivation. That makes rejection more personal, but of course it might not be about you. It could be about them.

Remember you don't know the conversations going on behind the scenes.

> 'We couldn't offer him the role. He wouldn't stay working for that nightmare of a manager for more than a month. He's way too good. He'd be out of here in six months and we need a plodder. We need someone who is far more antisocial for this role, he was just too nice to stick in a corner like we need them to.'

They can't write what's really going on in a job description for the whole world to see. It might be you, but it might not. Never let your self-talk limit you with unhelpful assumptions. What are you telling yourself? Have you got evidence for that? Could it be something else? What can you do to improve?

If your ratio of interviews to offers is worrying you, seek help with your presentation skills. As a rule of thumb, I expect people to be in at least six interview processes before they land a job offer. Of course, it can happen quicker but my point is that it isn't all about your performance on the day. You might be up against a strong internal candidate who could leave if they don't get offered the job and that would cause too much disruption. Or companies stop hiring, particular job roles get pulled because of leadership changes, or head-count freezes, budget cuts, political issues – all sorts of factors can prevent you getting a job offer. Prepare as much as possible, practically be ready to give a First 100 days presentation by the second interview, be your best self on the day and follow up appropriately. After that, it is beyond your control; reread The Smart Job Search Plan, in Chapter 2: *It's not About You; Zena's Smart Job Search Plan.* You need to be in parallel processes, not only one interview at a time. Keep going to first interviews until you have a signed contract in your hand. All these connections can be useful; even if the job isn't right for you now, these might be great contacts for the future.

This chapter busts the myths about writing your CV and LinkedIn profile and shows you how to write these, as well as application forms that really work.

CHAPTER 10

CVs and LinkedIn: Why are you telling them this?

2

We've looked at how recruiters screen CVs and you know you have to cram yours full of achievements, not your subjective interpretation of how good you are. It's hard to look objectively at your CV and LinkedIn profile to see what is going to stand out to potential employers. There is an art to getting your CV through the door. Get a friend or someone from outside your work or sector to read it. Ask them if they understand exactly what you do from reading it, especially if you want to change sectors. This chapter addresses CV's specifically but all these points also apply to your LinkedIn profile, as the following chapter expands on, with more detailed information to help you.

For example, the following dot point was taken from a real CV.
- Managing cost centre accounts, processing invoices, organising workshops and external exhibitions.

But what cost centre accounts, how many invoices, workshops teaching what to who and what external exhibitions?

This tells me nothing and I can't be bothered to work it all out. If you can't explain what you do to me, you won't be able to explain what you are doing when you work for me.

All job seeking, bland, vanilla documents don't work and neither do documents that are full of fluff. Aim for punchy ones that prove the value you can bring. If you feel proud and excited when you read your CV that's usually a give-away. The reverse is also true. Let's look at the myths we often hear about CVs

Myth 1: there is a standard format for a good CV

If your CV gets you interviews, then it is working. If it doesn't get you interviews then it is not working, even if someone tells you it's 'good'. (It's probably not tailored aggressively enough to the roles you are interested in). There is no such thing as a generic 'good' CV; you may not need a key skills section; you may want to put a very relevant hobby at the beginning of your work history; you may not need to put letters after your name; it all depends on the message you want to get across. There are no fixed rules.

There is a basic example at the end of this chapter. Word software has several good CV templates you can choose. Make sure the style is appropriate, more contemporary or classic according to the audience you are targeting. It's got to represent your brand. If you are worried about ageism, make sure your CV looks particularly contemporary.

Myth 2: you need several CVs because you have several options

You can only have one LinkedIn profile and your CV has to correlate with the identity you are building on LinkedIn. It's better to decide on the main expertise and goals for your next role and put all your focus into finding it, rather than having several weaker options while you hedge your bets. That just confuses recruiters who don't feel you are committed. You can always change your focus if Plan A doesn't work.

Each CV needs to be tailored to the role you are applying for. The personal statement explains what you bring to the new role and why you are interested in it. The work history needs case studies and successes that match the requirements of the job description. Have a master CV, which you adapt for each role. When you save your CV, use your name simply CVzenaeverett. Not Zenaeverettvs5, zenaCVsales, myCV, CV2016 or any other iterations that give away how long you have been on the market or that you may be considering more than one option.

2

Myth 3: you must send in your CV if you want to get a job
Your approach to job seeking has to mirror the way you conduct the rest of your working life. What is the most appropriate way to grab the attention of the people you want to work for? If you want a job at the cutting edge of design for example, is a dull old CV in a boring font really going to cut the mustard? Wouldn't you be better sending in examples of your designs? If you are a business developer, wishing to work for a competitive organisation, are you going to email their HR department a CV and application letter and wait for them to make contact? Or are you going to pick up the phone and call your potential boss; the way you would develop business in your day job?

Myth 4: it should be on only one page or two
It needs to be interesting and relevant. If you need to go to two or three pages, then do. The most read section is the first two thirds of the first page, but if you have particularly interesting and relevant employment history then include it. Interim and consultancy CVs need longer case studies to de relevant assignments. You may need to include publications or systems used.

Think; *'Why am I telling them this?'* for every single detail. If it's not relevant then take it out. If it's too waffly people will make the assumption you can't summarise or you can't see the big picture in the rest of your work either.

Keep it to a 12 or 11 font, in an easy to read sans serif font like Times New Roman, Arial or Cambria. Don't make it a smaller font to try and cram everything into two pages. I've also heard about a trick of putting key words in white in the background so your CV is optimised for online job boards. I have no evidence that this works but I know the search engines don't like it if you do it on websites. Your key words should occur naturally in the document. Don't be clever. Simply write great appealing content; headhunters are good at what they do; they'll find you.

Myth 5: It's more professional to hire an expert CV writer
I've touched on this already. Never pay someone else to write your CV; unless you need it translating into a different language. It is your document and your achievements and no one knows them as well as you do. It is immediately obvious at interview when someone's personality doesn't match the tone on the document; when they haven't written their own CV.

If you really can't write a basic CV, appropriate to the skill level required in the job you are applying for, that tells you something about other training you may need. A bit of help is fine of course, proofreading, reminders about what you have done, support with the formatting etc. but your CV needs to be written in your voice. Writing your CV helps you to put your career into perspective, so you know what you have achieved and can sell yourself better at interview. If you find writing your CV boring or overwhelming, you need support to change that attitude.

Myth 6: You don't want a recruitment agency changing your CV

You absolutely do, it's a good thing. It means they are working on you and sending your CV out to their clients. They will want to remove your contact details and maybe edit the CV to tailor it to their role. What's the problem with that? They aren't going to doctor it with incorrect information because that's a sure-fire way to lose their precious clients. Don't save your CV as anything other than a Word document to make it easier for them to edit and format it into their own layout. If their version isn't great, you can always explain it when you are in front of the client. Do make sure you know where they are sending it. Ask them who their contact is - by name ideally - and if it is going to more than one agency – who has suggested that organisation to you, say; *'Someone else has mentioned they can get me in there, can we agree if I don't hear from you in two weeks, I will let them try?'*

Myth 7: You need to include all your work experience

You don't. Don't have gaps – explain the sequence of your career history – but there is no need to explain all the detail of each role. If you've had a lengthy career you might want to call your employment section 'career highlights' and put the main relevant experience, tailored to the roles you are interested in. You can also put in summaries, for example, 'earlier career history' or 'prior to 1990' and bullet-point jobs.

Your CV is not a list of everything you have ever done in your working life: the trend is to produce a resume instead of a CV. It is a summary of your relevant career to sell you into your next employer and get you an interview. Many employers, such as the NHS or public sector, want full details of your whole career, which is why they give you an application form.

Myth 8: You need to include all your qualifications

You don't need to do that either. You put in the recent/most relevant ones. If you have a degree and ten years work experience why do they need to know your A level results?

2

Your professional qualifications are more relevant. Keep asking yourself; *'Why am I telling them this?'*

If you include out of date qualifications on your CV, such as CSEs, O levels, Pitmans Shorthand etc. it will show them that you are also out of date. Get rid of these points in your CV and show you are up for the challenges of the contemporary workplace, by emphasising your knowledge of current technology, systems, processes and regulations instead.

Myth 9: Nobody is interested in your hobbies
That might be because they are uninteresting (I like cooking, reading and walking my dogs, how dull is that?). Hobbies and extra-curricular activities can be useful to include if they are relevant to the role, or show you fit into a particular culture, or provide evidence of your personality, such as taking initiative. You design your own clothes and want to work as an accountant in the fashion industry for example, or you have organised fundraising events for charity and want to get a sales job. Showing energetic activities can counter age bias and mentioning success in team sports is evidence of team working, much better than saying you are a 'good team player'. If you are going to put it in this section, again think; *'Why am I telling them this, how is it relevant to the job?'* Make sure your passion comes across.

If your voluntary work or hobby is particularly relevant to the job you want to do next, include them in your current work experience so the recruiters' eye is draw to that first. This is important because it shows that what you do outside your day job provides the hooks or transferable skills you need to change careers. I had a client who put her Saturday vintage clothes stall at the top of her work history and put her formal marketing experience underneath it, which helped her move from a marketing job in financial services into one in retail. The Saturday job helped to provide a steppingstone from one context to another.

Like the rest of the document, if you are going to put something in this section explain it and make it relevant. The level of competition you play at, the results of your charity fundraising, the difference you made at the parent teachers association. If you cook; what food are you passionate about? If you read; is there a particular genre you prefer? That tells the recruiters more about your personality, your energy levels and how you will fit into an organisation. If you trained as a linesman rather than simply watching your child play a sport; it is evidence of your ability to go the extra mile.

Many people's advice is to leave out passions that other people might not share: your religion; favourite charitable causes; or the teams you support, for example. I think that if these are incredibly important to you, it is best to get them out on the table at the outset. If you will have a troubled relationship with your new colleagues because of a fundamental difference in values or opinions, it is better to find out at this stage than after you have signed a contract of employment.

In the same vein, you might want to mention your family in this section, rather than pretending you don't have any. If your firm is going to be un-family friendly it is better to screen yourself out at this stage. However, having said that as a recruiter, it can be rather nauseating and baffling when people include statements, such as; *'Spending time with my wife and children'* in the hobbies and interests section.

What you should never include on your CV

Your date of birth

Companies are not allowed to discriminate against you because of your age and for this reason you are not supposed to put your date of birth on your CV. Obviously, people can calculate your rough age by looking at your dates of employment or education if you include the dates you went to college etc.

Financial or personal information

Never include your bank details, national insurance number, passport number or any other confidential information. There have been examples of identity theft when this kind of detail is included on CVs put on job boards. Also, recruiters and potential employers don't want to know your children's names.

A picture

Recruiters don't like this in the UK. They can find your photo on your LinkedIn profile and from their online snooping. Get real, of course potential employers check you out, whether they are supposed to or not. Lock down your social media.

Your address

Many people tell you not to include your address. Most recruitment agencies will remove this anyway because they don't want potential employers contacting you directly. Most of us are easy to find online if someone tries hard enough. However, you might want to include your town and the first section of your postcode. This is so you show up on geographical searches. If you have a mobile phone include this number, people rarely ring landlines these days anyway. Also, there is the risk of a moody teenager/over friendly parent answering it.

On the subject of mobiles; make sure you have a personal answering message, not the factory default. Recruiters want to hear your voice and make sure they are leaving messages about potentially confidential vacancies on the right number. Also, they want to know you understand basic technology and can change a voicemail or have the charm to get someone to help you do so.

Sample CV content

There is a recommended template at the back of this book on page 298 for you to follow as a framework. Below are the finer details for you to consider and include, when you are ready.

Name

Email (professional address please, no funnies and a good email provider)

Mobile

Career Statement
What you have been doing; what you want to do next; the skills you have to bridge between the two. What can you do for the reader? As succinct as possible and specific! Use key words that match the job description if you are applying to a specific advertisement or want to come up in searches for specific job titles. You will probably have to adjust this slightly for each application.

Career History
Job Title
Company name, location
Dates, month and year, most recent first
Include a few lines to summarise the key responsibilities/accountabilities of your role perhaps some indication of the size of the organisation or department to put it into context.

Bullet pointed key achievements
What did you do over and above your job description?
What is your greatest legacy?
What will you be remembered for?

Repeat this for the full sequence of your working life

2

Other skills
For example:
- Computing: Advanced Microsoft Word, Microsoft Excel, Microsoft PowerPoint, Outlook, Lotus Notes
- Languages: Fluent French, working knowledge of Spanish

Education
Some people choose to put this before the career history

Date   **University name**
Degree
Perhaps anything relevant such as the subject of your dissertation

Date   **Secondary school name**
EG 3 A levels, 3 AS levels and 10 GCSEs (including Maths, English and Science)

Interests and Activities
Make these relevant to what you want to do if possible, particularly if you are changing careers. You can include voluntary work; or put it into your career history – whatever is most relevant to the reader.

Referees
You don't need to include these if you prefer not to, or if you need the space. Instead, you can include: *'Professional and personal references available on request.'* Generally, it is recommended not to give details of referees at this stage if you are posting your CVs on job boards.

Final points on writing your CV

What are the assumptions people make about your last company? You will also be judged on the company you have previously worked for; be mindful of the employer brand of your organisation. People make assumptions about you, based on where you work: what kind of corporate culture you will fit in to; the type of person you are; how you work; the type of support you might need etc. If you work in a large corporate, perhaps you couldn't adapt to a small business that hasn't got so many support functions. If you work in a highly unionised environment, could you move to a dog-eat-dog environment that is less patriarchal? If you work in the public sector, could you survive in a more entrepreneurial culture?

2

You can get round this by explaining what you do and where you work in a relevant way. *'My role is to provide accurate management data in a highly pressurised environment and under strict deadlines to enable the department managers to achieve their government targets.'* Or *'Fundraising in the charity sector is highly competitive and last year our organisation increased market share by 12.75%.'*

Bullet points or narrative

Both. Explain your role responsibilities as a narrative and bullet point detailed achievements, below the name of your current/last employer describe exactly what you do, in what context: the main purpose of your role; who your reported to; and a sense of scale.

For example
October 2013 – present day
Swarrods Ltd, Knightsbridge, London
Retail Manager (Menswear Department)

'Ran the entire menswear department of this luxury fashion store. Managed a team of 35 shop assistants, with two other assistant managers reporting to me. Reported to the Head of Menswear.'

Next, bullet-point your achievements underneath. They aren't interested in your job description; they can work out what that is. What they want to know is what you have achieved over and above your job description, such as;

'When I took over the department, it had a turnover of £50,000 per week. By improving merchandising and building closer relationships with the buying team, I trebled this figure within seven months.'

It's helpful to a recruiter to see the scope of your job, so they can figure out what your next likely move will be. They don't want to call a candidate and suggest a job that is way too junior – or senior – and risk a flea in their ear. Be specific about the context of your achievements. 'Managing a large team', 'achieving high profits' 'quickly' are all too vague. If you can't state the numbers because of confidentiality issues, you can at least compare your performance against target peers.

Start your bullet points with verb - action words – such as: started; built; pioneered; championed; led; began; and originated. The 'from – to' formula is preferable: 'when I took over the business it looked like this, now I have built it to X.' Don't be tempted to leave out important details like this in an effort to be concise. If it is relevant and interesting then they want to read it.

What is your message?

Once you have finished writing your CV, match it against the job descriptions that you are interested in applying for. Does it absolutely nail the application? Does it give evidence that you have done the same job before, in a similar context and that you can hit the ground running? A clever trick is to run it through a Word Cloud programme like Wordle – to see the key words it finds, you can do the same with the job description. Are the most prominent words the main competencies that you want to promote?

Top tips for completing application forms

Application forms are commonly used in the public sector and in corporate organisations who are looking for specific information rather than trawling through CVs. They can be really tedious to complete and if you don't match the main criteria then don't waste your time. These are volume recruiters looking for close matches of experience, not potential.

2

Here are several top tips to help you get short-listed.

- Usual rules of matching key words, phrases and their jargon apply.
- Mirror their language.
- Their jargon, not yours.
- Make sure you prove you have fulfilled the key responsibilities of the role at the top of the job description, rather than focusing on all the competencies they need.
- Maximum word count is critical, work within it. Give appropriate detail but be succinct: they'll be grateful. Keep your sentences short.
- Use headings and sub-headings and good paragraphs to make it easy to read.
- Make sure the document looks good, plenty of white space.
- If you are asked to provide referees, always seek their permission and give them an idea of the role responsibility so they know the angle you want them to take.
- Be careful if you are cutting and pasting from previous application forms, you don't want to submit a generic application.

- Print the form and check it before you send it out.
- Check your spelling, don't rely on spellcheck.
- Get a friend or your career coach to check it for you.
- If you can't get help, proof read it - from right to left and - then from left to right.

Supporting statements

I recently managed a CEO recruitment process for one of my clients. We asked the candidates to send in a CV and a brief supporting statement outlining what they could do for the organisation. It was a salutary lesson in why people need to face outwards rather than thinking about their own issues.

We didn't say that the longest supporting statement would be the winner, but that is clearly what some candidates thought. Many of these submitted statements occupied three pages, some were densely packed with a brain dump of everything the candidate knew about the sector, others included everything they had done since early childhood, some said what they thought the organisation was doing wrong. Some even treated it as an opportunity to write a mystery story, not mentioning they were applying for the job until the very last paragraph! I wanted to turn those into a murder mystery. Making the reader cross is not a good way to start. How arrogant to think recruiters would even bother to read all that. I am sure these weren't crazy people, but something flipped when they sat down to apply for this quite senior role.

A very few - the short-listed ones - addressed the issues being faced early in the document and succinctly said what they could do to provide a solution. They researched the business, made calculated guesses about the challenges and outlined what they could do for the organisation, explaining that they had done something similar already and the results they had achieved. They used headlines such as 'cost management', 'performance management' and 'current threats' which reflected the job specification they had received. The good ones rarely took up more than 1.5 pages. They had bullet points, lots of white space and headings and were easy to read. They clearly demonstrated that they could write a readable report that the organisation would want to read if they worked with them.

One particularly good one started with:
'I am grateful for the opportunity to apply for the role of Chief Executive Officer with XXX. My motivation for applying for this role is driven by my passion for reshaping the delivery of quality services and...'

One particularly irritating one started with:
'Overall, I feel I am a most suitable applicant for this position.'

Humility and a desire to serve, trumps arrogance any day.

Competencies for a Chief Executive include the ability to write concisely, deliver clear messages, quickly grasp issues and get their point across. Some candidates failed at the first hurdle by not demonstrating these abilities when they applied for the job. They showed they were good talkers; not good thinkers. They certainly weren't thinking about the organisation in question, it was all about them.

A simple exercise of stepping back, taking a highlighter to the job specification to emphasise the outputs needed and asking; *'What keeps this Board awake at night?'* would have prompted the required answers. The recruiters didn't want to know everything about them at this stage, that's what the interview is for. They wanted to know the candidates could read between the lines and fix the company's problems. No organisation can advertise their worries; but the clues are normally hidden in plain sight.

Incidentally, I didn't want to insult anyone by including the real basics here, but it is critical to get the recruiters or employer's name right. Gobsmackingly, though, in this case one person sent his email correctly to the HR Manager of the business, let's call her Mira. However, he then wrote to 'Dear Mary' in his email and again to 'Dear Mary' for good measure in his attached covering letter. He never managed to claw his way back from that. She'd have been reporting to someone who couldn't be bothered to check her name and worse still, preferred an anglicised version of it. The unconscious bias worked both ways in this case.

The other side of the coin as a recruiter is when you are faced with selecting a long list from a bunch of equally excellent CVs. In this case, a good personal statement makes all the difference. I was in this situation recently, for a non- executive role I was managing. I wondered why some of the candidates had applied because they seemed over-qualified for the job and almost intimidatingly good, which proves that you can't predict what recruiters think – we have our insecurities also. The statements that explained why these people were interested in the role and what they could contribute really made a difference.

One method of drafting a supporting statement is to use these headings below, with bullet point answers to each one underneath.
- Priorities of the role.
- What I can bring to it.
- Why I am interested in the role.

Ignore the closing date
Don't wait until the closing date to submit your application. Get it in as soon as possible. Ideally, be in pole (first) position, where the other candidates are being compared to you. Later on in the process the recruiters will stop remembering names and be less scrupulous in their filtering processes. It's not unknown for shortlists to be compiled before the closing date because the company risks losing active candidates. If the previous interview slots are all taken, you can be on the reserve list instead. It is a candidate's market after all – there is a shortage of great

people - so you have to grab them quickly. Some jobsites also charge per click – in other words you get charged every time a candidate applies for your job - regardless of whether they are a perfect fit or not. Sometimes companies pull the job advertisement down once they have tested the water. By the way, this is another reason why you can't assume that because there isn't an advertisement, there isn't a vacancy!

On the flip side, simply because the deadline has passed it doesn't mean they might not make an exception for you. Call them up, give them a plausible reason why you hadn't seen the advertisement until now and give them the most artful reason why they should see you that you can think of. Regardless of the answer, follow up with an email so they can find you if they want to. As ever, what have you got to lose?

2

This chapter will show you how to use LinkedIn and other social media opportunities in your job search and how to maximise the benefits of these platforms.

CHAPTER 11

Welcome to Netville: Social media

2

A well-written LinkedIn profile is a ubiquitous part of building your personal brand now, as well as a great way of staying in touch with previous colleagues. It's not only a job search tool; it's a great way for your colleagues, stakeholders, clients and customers to see exactly what your expertise is. Most profile views come from peers.

It's not enough to be good at your job these days. You have to be visible too. It's a global talent pool. It is not acceptable to have a lame profile these days, or to get your PA or PR department to write one for you. It helps to show that you are technically savvy by crafting an edgy profile, which portrays your years of experience as an asset, not a liability.

However, being on LinkedIn isn't enough, like any form of networking, online or in the real world, you get out what you put in. It's there to help you build relationships, as well as to be found. If you don't think it's relevant to your sector then make your own profile anonymous and have a good cyber-stalking session. Click on your small photo on the top right hand corner and go into the profiles and setting section to do that. You will be surprised at who you find. Also at the crapola (something useless or unimportant) you will find on some profiles too! It's a good idea to check out your peers anyway, to see that your keywords and terminology are up to date.

You don't need to pay for a premium service on LinkedIn if you use it properly. Build connections to broaden your reach and optimise your profile with the right keywords for your skills and experience. Never up load your CV – put in a summary and a few bullet points with main achievements - being mindful of any confidentiality and social media policies you have to follow. The same rules apply as in CV writing. Think; *'Why am I telling them this?'* Less is more. Too much detail looks desperate.

If you can, start building your LinkedIn network well before you need it to build business and peer relationships rather than job search ones. Obviously, you need to be more discrete about content if you are a passive i.e. working but open to opportunities job seeker, than if you are actively on the market. However, headhunters and recruiters will find you. That's what they do.

Six ways to use LinkedIn in your job search

1. To reconnect and connect with previous colleagues and anyone who might be able to help you, or give you leads, or recommend you.
2. To be found by headhunters and recruiters looking for someone with your skillset.
3. For headhunters and recruiters to look up when someone has given them your name and they don't have your CV.
4. As a companion to your CV, showing your photo so they can see what you look like and with recommendations so they know how good you are.

5. For the job function, which gives you great clues as to which firms are hiring in your area and active recruiters in your function/sector/region, even if the jobs aren't right for you.
6. To research companies and interviewers.

Ten latest LinkedIn tips

1. Get your headline right to make yourself visible

LinkedIn has more than 450 million members, averaging two new ones every second and their goal is to have 3 billion. That's a lot of profiles for recruiters to search through! To make yours visible it is imperative that you get your details right. Work backwards. If you were a recruiter searching for someone like you in LinkedIn, what is the job title, industry sector and key words you would use? Your profile needs to match this. When you type in your most recent/current job LinkedIn builds a default headline for you based on what your current job title is. You can change this and sometimes people use several job titles to make sure they catch all the options. Put in all the titles of the roles you are applying for, for examples; Finance Business Partner | FP & A Manager | Head of Divisional Finance.

The modern polymath fits all his job titles in his headline, rather than having several profiles, for example; Leonardo Da Vinci: Painter | Sculptor | Architect | Musician | Mathematician | Inventor | Scientist | Engineer | Botanist | Cartographer

The point is, no one searches for: Immediately Available or Actively seeking a New Opportunity. These are counter-productive.

You are only allowed to put in one industry. Make sure you choose the correct one, possibly what you want to do next. Your location is where you want to work. If you live in Southampton and want to work in Manchester, then put Manchester as your location.

2. Include a photo on your profile

LinkedIn says you are seven times more likely to be contacted if you have a profile photograph. You look completely digitally challenged by not having one. It means you have something to hide or you can't work out how to upload a photo. Get a picture of you at your professional best, taken after a trip to the hairdressers if it makes you feel better. Recruiters don't have time now to meet with candidates speculatively and they want to see what you look like from your profile. That means you by the way, not your logo. A sporting one can be ok, but not the Christmas party. It depends on the image you want to portray.

Put a panoramic background on your profile that backs up what you want to be seen as doing. This is slightly easier if you are in a more creative industry, but you can still have fun with it, to reflect the sector you work in, or where you work.

3. Craft your profile to reflect your message

Only you can post on your LinkedIn page. You can't get tagged as you do in Facebook. You can switch the position of the boxes to suit your message. The summary section has 52 lines and you can include key projects, or type in what your customers say about you, anything that helps. If you want to do something different; explain why and put your skills in there, as well as the skills section.

If you are making minor changes then switch off 'send to network' because it is counterproductive for them to see lots of small changes. Switch it back on for bigger changes that you want your network to see, such as adding new recommendations. Keep it simple. It's a summary.

4. Build relationships by engaging with people

It's a networking site. So, network! It's not enough just to be on LinkedIn; you have to work it. Research shows it's not your connections who are the most likely source of future work; it's your connections' connections. The more ex-colleagues, peers, past employers, suppliers, old friends, university mates, people you meet at conferences and you connect with, the better. Do not transfer your whole contacts list on to LinkedIn, of course. Use old-fashioned manners in a digital medium. Congratulate people, endorse them, comment on posts, share interesting information that reflects your wisdom and expertise etc.

5. Build connections with recruiters

Sometimes recruiters or their researchers will look at your profile and see if you respond. Or they send you an invitation to connect. They may be making a first approach to see if you are potentially interested in a conversation with them. Don't connect with all of them, but if they look interesting you could send them an in mail or message in return, for example; 'I saw you looked at my profile, any particular reason?' It's ok to be connected to good recruiters in your sector. Successful people have those relationships. It doesn't mean you are on the market; you could be a client of theirs or they could (shock horror) even be friends of yours. And is there any harm in keeping your organization on its toes by thinking you are dipping your toes in the market?

If you are worried that recruiters are using you to go through your connections, make them invisible so they can only see your mutual connections. However, some people think we should all share our networks and will disconnect with connections that don't share: but it's your choice. They won't disconnect with you if you are good or influential.

6. Send personal invitations

Don't send a generic untailored request to link. You will find people might not bother. Generic communication means you are missing an opportunity to engage and explain why a particular individual would benefit from being connected to you. You wouldn't give someone a business card at a networking event without some conversational preamble. It is the same principle here. Say something about what you have in common, or something complimentary. What's in it for them to be

2

connected to you? If you are connecting via a smartphone you don't have the option of a personal message. Don't do this if you don't already know the person.

Connections are just that. They're not friends or people you recommend, merely people who help you to reach out further. You want a balance of quantity and quality for the algorithms to work. Similarly, accept invitations from people you don't know if they work for organisations you are interested in, or if they have access to an interesting network.

If you are sending connections to friends then tick 'we've done business together.' Especially, when you are relying on them for recommendations; that looks much more professional.

7. Receive and give recommendations

In an era when most organisations won't give any detail on references, it's amazing that people are still allowed to make such gushing recommendations on LinkedIn. These are a big help in backing up the evidence on your profile. Get recommended and make judicious recommendations. Never make reciprocal recommendations; they look contrived. The more senior the recommendation the better and you can also invite other stakeholders, such as suppliers, to do the same. When your clients say that you are the best account manager they've ever had it makes you very attractive to competitors.

As most people find it easier to edit rather than compose, you might want to request a recommendation suggesting what you would like them to say 'I really want to focus on designing magazine covers in future, so if you could say that your best selling editions last year all featured my covers, that would be enormously helpful.'

Also, give other people recommendations, subtly promoting your own message too; 'Customer service is at the heart of what we do at Legs & Co and Darren really reflected this in the way he managed our new business.' Volunteer recommendations for suppliers who are active on LinkedIn, or customers, if you want your market to know you work with them. If you are a senior individual then people asking you for references is an indicator of your management success.

8. Think skills

This section is where your peers review your skills. The more endorsements you have, the higher up the search functions you go. Choose your own, don't rely on the ones LinkedIn suggests for you and make sure that you are searchable for the right key words. Again, the more specific the better; not 'leadership' or 'management', but specifics: Business Continuity Management, Asset Recovery, Loan Management, Sanctions Laws, Six Sigma, LEAN, for example. Also, endorse your connections' skills, to remind them you exist.

9. Share value

Frequently update your profile by adding articles, blog posts, presentations and other interesting content to your activity stream. Find information that is helpful to your connections and they may wish to share with their own connections: a great way to 'up' your visibility. See what they comment on or share or 'like.' This is feedback for you about what they think is important. Your updates should reflect your specialist interests or expertise so people 'get' what it is you can do for them. Avoid overt plugging. Read your network's activity feeds and comment on them. This will help you build stronger connections. LinkedIn even provides you with relevant content to share via its powerful news aggregator, LinkedIn Today. 'Like' news and articles to remind your network you are there also, but be genuine. You can spot when someone is doing something for the sake of it, such as sharing too many articles at once.

10. Join groups and follow companies – with caution

Demonstrate that you keep up with trends by joining relevant groups and participating in discussions. LinkedIn lets you

2

message people in the same group, even if you aren't directly connected to them. However, be careful about joining too many groups and following too many companies and avoid getting daily emails; they can be time wasters. Hide any Career Groups as it implies you are actively looking for a job and remember you can choose which of your groups are visible. Some recruiters in some sectors avoid active job seekers. Their clients pay them to tease out talent - not pick CVs off job boards – so manage your brand image.

LinkedIn is a fantastic tool but not a panacea. I think the sooner you get off it, on to personal email and then face to face, the better. We don't want you hiding behind screens for too long; merely use this tool to start a conversation and research leads.

Facebook, Instagram, Twitter and other social media

Mind Flipping means proving how valuable you are to future employers by demonstrating your previous achievements in an evidence based way. How you provide that evidence obviously depends on what it is and your potential audience. If you are in a creative industry, you need to be creative in how you do it. Sending a dull CV is unlikely to be enough to get you a job as a photographer/creative designer/dress maker/chef and so on. Building a relationship with your potential employer or user of your freelance services on Instagram, by making genuine (not contrived) comments on their posts so they start following you, is a clever way to do this. You still need to get in front of people, but this is another way to start the conversation. The art is choosing the right tool to become visible to them and relating to them in their language.

Jess's Success Story

I had a client who worked in a small, slightly chaotic, PR agency and wanted to move into a large organization and have a 'proper' corporate career. Jess and I had our first session in a hotel near her office. We were discussing if she could discretely approach some of her clients to suss out job opportunities with them - the Poacher Turned Gamekeeper Move - when she took a sip of her coffee and made some comment about how well the bean had been roasted. It turned out she was passionate about coffee, could do blind tastings and had even travelled to South America to visit coffee plantations in her gap year. Jess said she would love to work in that industry but had no obvious experience for the consumer sector and couldn't afford to live on a barista's salary. She had applied for jobs with coffee manufacturers and distributors but had been rejected (no 'hooks' for them: they looked at her most recent job, PR for professional services companies and understandably saw no relevance). She was following her favourite firms on social media but that's not enough. We decided on a strategy to, well, get her in their face.

Jess started to engage with them on Twitter. Twitter feeds are often managed by the corporate communications department; the internal equivalent of PR. Over a couple of months, they got to know her and her passion and knowledge of their product. She sent them a direct message, explaining that she would love to work in the coffee industry and had skills in writing and networking with journalists that could be useful. At the same time, things got too much in her agency and she resigned (thinking she'd try that barista's salary for a bit after all). A maternity contract role came up for an Internal Communications Manager position, she was interviewed for it and got the offer. The role was never advertised because they knew Jess was available immediately. She hasn't yet managed to get out of the communications department into a buying role – her ultimate goal – but she's in the right place.

As ever, it is all about thoughtful use of the best way of engaging with your potential client/employer. Following them on social media helps you to understand them better and work out where the gaps are that you can fill. You can see how they present their employer and consumer brands, follow their feeds, read what their customer's say about them and how they interact with those customers. Are there gaps in their product offering? Have their clients complained about part of their service? Who are their customers and what do they want?

Again, social media is one tool that can be more or less helpful depending on the role you do. If you are using it is as part of your job - you need to walk the talk - by using it as part of your job search. If you have any kind of customer interaction, it is likely that social media will be part of your research.

Patrol your own profile

The other side of the coin is that social media will be part of a future employer's research on you. They will check you out early in the process - to avoid explanation/embarrassment/litigation later on - so manage your own digital footprint and check yourself out.

Pop your name into Google and see what comes up. Your LinkedIn profile is well optimised and there is your Facebook profile early on the page too. Experiment with your mobile number also: that can lead you to other links. A headhunter contact of mine says she always looks for a candidate's Facebook page and if she can't find it, she tries putting in their mobile number. It sometimes works.

Facebook is the main worry. Take down anything inappropriate, or at the very least shut down your page and all your albums so only your connections can see anything. Remove your tags from other people's pages that show you in an unhelpful light; or any light that doesn't represent the brand you want. You can adjust your privacy settings so you can review photographs you have been tagged in before they are used. And watch your partner's/ children's profiles. If people know their names (you mention them at interview for example) they can check their profiles and oh... there are silly photos of you on there too. Make sure their privacy settings are at the highest levels, the same as yours.

Check all your comments, tweets and videos. YouTube is easy to overlook, but don't forget to check it also.

This isn't only about over-sharing kitten videos, off-putting though that is. For example, a couple of years ago I was contacted by someone who wanted my help because he wasn't getting many interviews, despite having a good CV. When he did get interviews, the jobs kept being pulled. He felt he was being given excuses; the bank had decided not to hire at this stage and so on. He was frustrated and perplexed. While I was speaking to him I popped his name into Google. There he was, on YouTube, singing sickening racist songs outside London landmarks. Horrible. Not only was he racist, he was a particularly stupid racist. You can see why people do a search on future employees. We put out our digital footprint, and we have to take the consequences of what people find out about us.

2

This chapter will help you to connect with new networks and learn how network without 'Networking!'
Also known as painless networking.

CHAPTER 12

Birds of a feather flock together; painless networking

Nearly all my clients find work through their networks, or more usually their network's network. By networking, I mean getting out there and talking to people about what you do and the value you bring to create opportunities. This can be at formal networking events, but also in the general course of your everyday life.

In their fascinating book on social networks, Connected, Nicholas Christakis and James Fowler explain that although we are connected to everyone else by six degrees of separation, their research shows that word of mouth recommendations follow a Three Degrees of Influence Rule, beyond which your influence dissipates. This means: your contacts; your contacts' contacts; and your contacts' contacts' contacts; are all within your reach.

However, the stronger your network the broader your sphere of influence. If you have twenty business connections and they in turn have twenty business connections each - let's assume different connections to you - then that means you are indirectly connected to four hundred people at two degrees of separation. That's a lot of potential opportunities to explore.

This explains why new opportunities often come from surprising sources, such as talking to other parents at the touchlines at weekends. I had a client who was a Business Development Manager in the financial services industry. He had a couple of hours commute into the City of London and really wanted to find a local job. He was chatting to another parent while watching their boys play football match and she turned out to be in a senior role in a local consumer goods business. The Sales Director wanted to win new contracts supplying into the financial services industry and she set up a meeting between the two. He hadn't advertised the position, but he had a problem he needed to solve. You've guessed the rest. It was a classic, Zena Poacher Turned Gamekeeper Move – they wanted him for his understanding of the financial services industry and because of his network. He wanted to get out of his industry but knew he needed to leverage it to take the first step out. Once he was in the consumer industry he could develop a new client base. The Three Degrees of Influence Rule worked to get him there.

'The spread of influence in our social networks obeys the Three Degrees of Influence Rule. Our influence gradually dissipates and ceases to have a noticeable effect on people beyond the social frontier that lies at three degrees of separation.'

Nicholas Christakis and James Fowler, Connected, (2010)

Build your cultural capital

Of course, social mobility comes into this because many of us have better networks than others and start with an unfair advantage. I want to make it clear that I am not only talking to stereotypical middle class families who can get themselves and their kids on the right path. We all know the advantages of cronyism; from helicopter parents doing homework, to unpaid internships in middle class careers, to influential models. Where do you start if you don't have this? Employers want people with fire in their bellies who can think on their feet. If you don't have the advantage of a network, there has still got to be someone, somewhere who can be useful to you. Generally, once my clients are clear on what they want to do next, useful contacts start to come to mind. LinkedIn is a big help in identifying possible connections so milk it to find out who you know.

2

Christakis and Fowler talk about *homophily*, the conscious or unconscious tendency to associate with people who resemble us. The word literally means 'love of being alike.'

'Usually, members of the majority hold most of the powerful positions and the people who get to know them also tend to be from the majority.'

Arnold, 2003

'Job opportunities go to people they know so these social networks become self perpetuating.'

Ibarra, 1995

Once people understand how to sell their value, they feel more valuable and this gives minority candidates the courage to try and break these majority networks. Learning to Mind Flip is a tool to make yourself the indispensable candidate and break through the network.

Connect with people who share your interests, values, passions and goals. You may not have a common history, but you are one of them through your shared work or expertise and your passion to do well. Your enthusiasm will help you build connections with like-minded people who are also on their way up, or who are already in a position of influence. You need just one well-connected contact or mentor who can connect you to their network, who in turn will connect you onwards through their network. Build up your cultural capital; look and behave like you belong. Don't be frightened of applying to selective institutions or organisations because you are nervous about fitting in: you are building barriers to your own success by doing that.

A common characteristic I have observed in successful people is that they are happy to support other ambitious people. They know great goals can be achieved because they have achieved them themselves. Avoid small-minded negative people who don't share your belief in the power of hard work, ambition and powerful goal setting. How we think is contagious; look at the difference a positive football team manager makes. You get what you expect in life and part of that is what other people expect from you too. Mind Flipping means controlling the perception other people have of you. You are a valuable person with a valuable contribution to make.

Strong mentors make a difference. We all need more mentoring relationships where members of a powerful majority take responsibility for developing the careers of other people who would normally be outside their network. Organisations want to tap into a broad talent pool; work this to your advantage and get in front of people who can give you a leg up.

Who is an obvious connection, you haven't tried yet?

If your ideas are drying up; think about whom you haven't tried yet. When I started in recruitment someone told me the right candidate for the job is usually right under your nose. In the same vein, usually leads for work are also right under your nose. Never over-complicate your job search. For example, should you reconnect with previous employers, previous colleagues, your friend's parents and people at church?

When you are talking to potential sources of work, be clear on your skillset, the value you add and leave the clear impression you are a no-brainer to bring into their business. Using these techniques will help people get round the 'jobs for the boys' culture and subconscious bias for people 'not quite like us' that they might come up against in some industries.

I believe most people like to help other people and give high potentials a leg up. And this isn't always altruism. Some companies pay substantial referral fees to their employees if they recommend people for internal vacancies.

2

Your appearance talks

It's a wise investment to build your network, even if you aren't on the market for a new move immediately. From now on, you are open to opportunities. Make it your business to look and sound like you are already fulfilling the job title you are aiming for and that you will fit in to the culture you want to work in.

Graduates, you might think your personality is reflected in the way you present yourself. In most industries however, there is a uniform way of dressing and if you don't conform you simply won't get in. When you are in employment, in a position of influence, you can work on changing the culture, but for now you want to blend in and be one of them. Your network will do you favours, but not if they damage their own relationships if you let them down. Don't narrow down your options.

David Schwarz in *The Magic of Thinking Big* says to never leave home without feeling certain you look like the kind of person you want to be. Your appearance talks; be sure it says positive things about you. People want to feel confident they can recommend you to their treasured contacts. If you look as good as you can; you feel as good as you can and that is infectious.

I once refused to interview a graduate who wanted my company to find him a job in the recruitment industry. He sounded ok on the phone but turned up to the office in a dirty T-shirt and jeans. Also, he was unshaven and this was long before the hipster beard trend. I felt if he couldn't be bothered to make an effort to meet me, he wasn't going to be bothered to make an effort for my clients either. If we managed to find him a job, I wasn't sure he had the drive to survive the long hours and tough targets that trainee recruiters face. We all make assumptions about people in the first couple of minutes. I gave him the option to think about it and make another appointment if he wanted to come back again; looking like I could send him straight out to meet a client. He did exactly that. We placed him, he worked in London for an accountancy recruitment agency who eventually transferred him to their Sydney office. I'm not sure if he still hates me but it was a good lesson.

Schwartz says your physical exterior represents your mental interior. You don't need to spend a fortune - although his advice is to buy half as many clothes but spend double on what you do buy - but dress appropriately and be as groomed as you can. Use the dry cleaners and polish your shoes. I am avoiding gender stereotyping, but at my age a pair of Teresa May heels and a manicure are priceless confidence boosts.

Never create obstacles to your own social mobility

'Most people live in a very restricted circle
of their potential being.'

The father of American Psychology, William James, 1842 - 1910

Mind Flip is all about smashing these circles. I have noticed how kids from poorer families are creating mental obstacles that get in the way of their career options. Bright children from poorer backgrounds appear not to have the confidence to break into top professions and universities. Don't let your own mind be your greatest obstacle to your success.

Organisations are missing out on the talents of bright people from poorer backgrounds who should be upwardly mobile, but are nervous of entering the middle-class world of the professional jobs market. They have the educational qualifications, but feel they won't fit in to perceived middle class career paths. They avoid potential rejection by not putting themselves forward. These days businesses are much more aware of bias in their selection processes, but they still miss out on good candidates if those 'different' candidates they are trying to attract won't give them a chance. That's a tragedy for all concerned.

2

In 2014, the Head of Policy at the Social Mobility and Child Poverty Commission, said that bright children from poor homes are less likely to apply to top universities because they are worried about 'not fitting in'. It's not just about education, where the politicians put all their focus; it is also about feeling 'comfortable' in middle class settings. He said, and this makes uncomfortable reading, that to succeed they need to become more comfortable with middle-class social settings such as restaurants, theatres and offices. Otherwise, children from poorer backgrounds write themselves off by not applying to the more selective universities or organisations. He said there is a lack of effective networks and advice to help navigate this new alien middle class world, which makes it more difficult for even the smarter students to translate their academic attainment into success in the professional jobs market.

Sir John Major, the former head of the Conservative Party, has warned that it was 'truly shocking' that private school educated and affluent middle-class children still run Britain (*The Daily Telegraph*, 3 March 2014). We'll never break the cycle of having the 7% of privately educated children fill a disproportionate number of powerful roles, if we don't raise the aspirations of young people from working class backgrounds.

Flip your mind if you can: think about the contribution you can make by pushing yourself forward. Stop worrying about your insecurities, find role models and mentors and milk those networks and schemes designed to help people like you. They do exist, check out this link to a Daily Mail article complaining that some public sector internships are skewed in your favour: http://www.dailymail.co.uk/news/article-1370567/Middle-class-youngsters-barred-internships-Whitehall-police-white.html).

It's possible you might not fit in, but it is also possible that you might. You might even fit in brilliantly. Park your insecurities and get out there. Confidence comes from action, not the other way round. Start by networking: you only need one or two people to open doors for you.

Quantity not quality in the early networking stages

When you start your job search, approach as many organisations as possible and have as many conversations as possible. Help can come from surprising sources, rather than always from the people you expect will be most useful to you. Obviously, if you are employed you will of course, have to be more discrete.

Imagine you were a trainee insurance salesman in the 1980s. The first thing they got you to do was to write out a list of 100 of your contacts, so you could sell your nearest and dearest a policy. Life is easier now we have databases and social media lists and obviously, in this situation now, LinkedIn is a great place to start. However, you should capture a list of everyone you know not only obvious business networking connections.

Possible source of jobs, leads and referrals

- Your school, university, MBA, training, or college contacts
- Current colleagues
- Past colleagues who have left your organisation
- Past and current colleagues of family members
- Consultants and interims who have worked in your business
- People who you used to work for
- People who used to work for you
- People in previous organisations you have worked for
- Sponsors/mentors – formal and informal relationships
- Members of business associations, unions, groups
- Business associates
- People you have met on trips or conferences
- Your suppliers – solicitors, auditors, salespeople, estate agents, recruiters – everyone you give business to
- Other people in your building
- Your customers and their customers
- Your friends, their friends and colleagues
- Your family, their friends and colleagues
- Your neighbours, people in your street/village
- The parents and staff at your children's school
- People you meet through your golf club or your children's sports clubs
- People at your hairdressers, barbers, nail bar
- Church or other religious group contacts
- People you know through other interests and hobbies
- Your drinking buddies
- Dog walking buddies, horse riding buddies
- People at the gym, your SPIN class, etc, etc
- Companies that want to be bought by your last employer
- Companies that want to do business with your last employer
- Companies with failed bids/tenders to work with your last employer

2

This is not an exhaustive list and some entrants may look a bit silly. The point I am labouring is that potential job leads can come from a variety of sources, not simply advertised roles. You probably know many more people than you realise.

Go through the list and think about what they do and what their partners or family connections do. Draw up a list of people to approach.

Business Associates are often one of the most helpful sources. Figure out who has a vested interest in getting you back to work; clients, customers you have looked after, auditors, suppliers, lawyers, recruiters etc. These are often a good source of market information and introductions. Do they have connections in businesses where they know that their needs will be looked after better if you are there, or that they will get business if you join a new firm? Who owes you favours? Buy coffees/beers and again, get out and network. Keep current in your market so you find out who has business problems you can solve.

The obvious Poacher Turned Gamekeeper Move
Who wants you as a direct consequence of the organisation you are working in or worked for most recently? Competitors? Clients? Potential suppliers? It usually pivots around this. Organisations who want to sell into your company? Or that have the same customers or use the same systems? Who should you be talking to that you haven't thought of already?

Tips for formal networking events
I've met very few people who really enjoy going to formal networking events. I run training courses on how to network and I dislike them myself. I have tried various strategies – including a glass of wine in the pub next door beforehand – and here's my advice on how to enjoy them.

- Only go if you are genuinely interested in the subject matter. Going along simply to network looks false. Networks are held together by trust. You've blown it from the start if you are there from a position of self-interest.
- It is better to come out with only one business card of someone you want to keep in touch with, than with a fistful of cards from working the room superficially.
- If you dislike networking, get to the event on time and start to chat to people as they arrive, including making yourself known to the organisers. Getting there later, when everyone is already in a conversation can be more daunting.
- If you go with a friend or colleague don't talk to them all night. Tempting though it is to stick together, it's not really the point. Chat to other people first and regroup at the end of the event.
- If you are out of work, but have known expertise, conference organisers can be keen for you to come. They sometimes give away free tickets, particularly if you will participate in panel discussions etc. It's a great way to stay current.
- Ideally, get a guest list before the event so you can target people to talk to. Don't make it obvious that you are there to talk to them, but get into conversation naturally with them. Here is an example.
  'Oh, Jane Smith, how lovely to meet you in person. My name is Zena and I was reading about your Women in Business group; such a great initiative in your industry. How's it progressing?'
- Describe what you do using the structure from your personal statement. Paint a visual picture of what you do so they remember you when talking to organisations who need what you do. Here are several examples.
  'I am on gardening leave from Oplus Lawyers. I've had seven great years there but really want to spend all my time doing data privacy work now, so I am chatting to some firms in town about that. The market seems quite good actually…. What about you?'

2

'I'm going back to work having been at home with the kids for a couple of years. My plan is to start again in September working for a smallish firm in an operational role. I used to work in advertising and I'd love a really busy creative environment, somewhere where everyone is a bit frazzled and they need some systems and processes.'

Never say.

'Well, I am out of work at the moment, so I am open to ideas. I am not going to think of people I know and say 'do you need anyone to work for you, I met this nice woman, not sure what she does but she is keen to go back to work and seems to be struggling a bit.'

- Listen. You don't learn by talking. You learn by listening. And people love to talk about their problems, so draw them into the conversation. Ask questions such as; *'What do you think should be done about such-and-such?'* or *'What do you think about X?'* Talk about the subject of the networking event. By asking questions – and actually listening to the answers – people will like you more and you will learn information that could be valuable.

- Next time you go to a networking event, pay attention to who is really listening to the conversation. Not many: they are preoccupied with looking over your shoulder to see if there is someone better they should speak to. Or else they appear desperate to speak over the person and thrust their opinion on them. That is not the way to build relationships or garner favours.

- Don't overdo the alcohol. It's easy to drink more than you intend to, particularly, if you haven't eaten beforehand; the canapés are frugal and your wine glass gets topped up frequently. I know when I get to the stage of thinking I am particularly scintillating company; it's time to catch the tube home.

- Send people LinkedIn invitations after the event and stay in contact, including a personalised message that refers to your conversation. For example. *'It was lovely to meet you last night and to get your opinions on Y. It would be good to connect on here and stay in touch.'*
- If your sector is quite traditional, have business cards printed, if you don't have them already, you can give out your contact details. Make sure you state your area of expertise. Present yourself confidently as an expert in whatever you do: social media strategy expert; global mushroom farming expert; cupcakes beyond your wildest dreams expert etc.
- Do some favours for them if you can. Networking is about playing it forward.

2

How to work out what their problem is and be the solution

Do as much research as you can and read between the lines. You know that job specification's often don't bear any resemblance to the real job. The most important point is right at the top of the document: the role responsibility. After that everything gets added on so the employee can't sue them for making them do a task that isn't in their job description. Focus on exactly what they want you to do and think about the following factors.

- What aren't they telling you?
- Is any of this in code? For example, a customer service job that involves hitting targets is really a sales job; tell them about your sales experience.
- What is really going on with this employer/team/organisation/person?
- What are the real issues here; not what their communications people write on the website?
- What is the most important part of the job description or brief and why does it matter?
- What can't they write in the job description that you should figure out?

- What is the biggest impact they want someone to make?
- What are the consequences of this not happening?
- What are their common problems and pain points?
- What do they worry about in the middle of the night?
- Of all the results they are asking for, what are the most important?
- If you were hiring someone for this position, what are the skills and experience you would look for?
- What is your matching evidence to show you have these skills and experience, that you have achieved the same outcomes in a similar context?

Cold calling and direct approaches when you haven't got a contact

This is often advised because it puts you in the driving seat: you have identified organisations you could add value to and now need to get on their radar. However, it is hard to do. It's difficult to get in front of companies these days without an introduction or lead in. Busy Board members know you won't waste their time. However, I've seen this work with smaller organisations or local businesses who are more likely to be flattered, by receiving direct approaches and pleased to know good talent is available on their doorstep.

Never assume that because they aren't advertising a job that is right for you, that they wouldn't be interested in your skillset.

It could be that someone is underperforming, but they won't do anything about them unless they know there is a good person (you) waiting in the wings. Or, you could solve a problem that they don't wish to advertise that they have: IT Director required who can get to grips with our erratic international payment system that threatens our relationship with our European supply chain. I don't think so!

I wouldn't recommend going to the HR Director first. Most of them will only respond if your CV matches a current vacancy, rather than viewing you as a potential fit for a future opportunity. Go as high up the chain as possible to the person with the problem in the business; a Functional Head or the person you would report directly to. www.ceoemail.com is a useful tool for finding email addresses and of course, you can find names through LinkedIn. This has worked for my clients when they have sent a pretty blunt email explaining what they do and how they could contribute. They don't always attach a CV, but may include a link to their customised LinkedIn url on their email signature. Contacts who have hired in this way have told me they generally ignore unsolicited emails, particularly if they are long and waffly; but occasionally if a punchy one comes across their desk they will take time to meet that person. They might not have anything immediately, but they refer them elsewhere if they can.

2

One of my contacts got a Board level job at a top retail company, a competitor of the one he was working at, by sending the CEO a letter. He thought a personal letter would have more impact than a CV that would be screened by his staff before it got to him. It worked, he might have been in the right place at the right time, but he got through the gatekeeper and his letter got a positive reply.

Selling your story

Hit them between the eyes with exactly what you can do for them. There isn't a whisker of room for any flannel here. Paint a picture of what you do; anchor it straight into what their problem is/where their business needs are and say you want to talk about it. You aren't asking for a job. You are looking for an opportunity to help/contribute. Here are several examples.

'I am a Sales Trainer, specialising in getting rookie pharmaceutical sales people to hit their revenue targets. I read in the Sunday Times that you are growing a pipeline of trainees and I'd love to talk to you about how I can contribute to their performance.'

'I am a Marketing Manager with particular expertise in understanding how high networth individuals in Europe and Asia purchase luxury brands online. Can I talk to you about your Hanson range and how I might help you develop these relationships?'

'I am a Generalist HR Director with extensive experience in building high-performing teams of unionised shift workers in the energy sector. There are synergies with the rail industry; I wondered if you had any opportunities for someone with my experience?'

The usual advice is not to go to HR but if the organisation states clearly on their careers page that you should, then do it. Phone as well and build relationships with the resourcing team so they know you. Never give up. The first call is hard but it gets easier. Simply because you have sent in your CV once doesn't mean it won't get lost; or that your contact is still working there. At least the company knows you exist. What have you got to lose? If they do respond with a 'thanks but nothing at the moment' you might ask them if there are any particular headhunters or recruiters they recommend you get in touch with. You are far more likely to get airtime with a recruiter; if you have been referred to them by a precious client.

Look out for movers
Keep an eye out for information about new hires in your sector. New Chief Executives and senior management often want to gain quick wins by bringing in new talent. Or, they give it a few months, assess the current staff and bring in their own people to

replace them. Sometimes their PR statements can give you clues as to their focus. Here is an example.

'Simon brings a wealth of valuable connections from his long career in advertising and will play a pivotal role in expanding our business.

Email Simon congratulating him on his great career move and point out you are a new business developer who could bring new contracts to the business, safe in the knowledge that under his leadership the firm will do an excellent job of delivering your clients' objectives. It's not about you, it's about Simon, the business and the clients. Flattery can work.'

2

How to get a recruiter to introduce you

When you really feel confident to go directly to your target organisation, get a recruiter to introduce you. The easiest way to find out which consultancies they use is to ring up the HR or recruitment team and ask them. Say you are from their sector, have admired the talent they have hired and ask which recruiter they use. Phone the recruiter, explain you want to be introduced, what you can do for the organisation and would they be prepared to meet you to discuss? It's a bit cheeky, but in my experience the more confident you sound about the value you add, the more your chance of being introduced. Even retained recruiters do these 'lob ins' where they introduce speculative candidates to organisations they have a close relationship with, so they don't miss out on talent. Other recruiters do speculative introductions to build relationships; it doesn't matter to you, you just want to get in there.

This chapter provides you with the best questions to ask interviewers; interview closing techniques; and tricks to negotiate the deal you want on your terms.

CHAPTER 13
Close the deal

2

We've talked about how you open an interview and how you present your achievements using STAR or CAR statements. The next difficult task is asking the interviewers questions. This also applies to when you are networking and creating opportunities for yourself outside a formal interview process.

The clichéd question is; *'Can you tell me what training and development plans are in place?'* If you are in a career, where we are talking about your experience rather than your potential, then they aren't there to train you. The best or worst one I've heard is; *'How many days can I have off sick before I need to produce a sick note?'*

Want to see some puppies?

You are aiming for a puppy dog close: the person at the other side of the desk is imagining working with you and dumping their problems on you and by the end of the interview doesn't want you to leave. The puppy dog close is when a sales person gives the prospect an opportunity to trial the product or service before the deal is closed. The prospect of course, doesn't want to give up that cute puppy and the puppy closes the deal. This principle applies to you going in the back door as a temporary or a consultant and creating a permanent opening. The company has work but doesn't want to risk a permanent hire, or they have a recruitment freeze; technically there are no openings. However, they have work to do and can bring in extra resources when needed. You become that cute puppy who they don't want to lose and you are the first one to be hired when there is a permanent opening. Sometimes managers with no openings will go out of their way to create an opening for an outstanding temporary worker.

Ask questions that uncover the realities of the role

Now is the time to understand the challenges and expectations of the role and align these with your own career goals and expertise. Interviews of course, are a two-way process. External hiring can go wrong because the incoming candidate doesn't understand the realities of the role, which may bear little resemblance to the job description. By the time they have understood the true picture it can be too late for both parties.

This is your chance to probe: asking about strategy; operations people; and processes.

Great questions to ask

- If you were taking this role, what would your priorities be?
- What do you expect me to achieve in my first three months?
- Who are the main stakeholders I need to influence?
- Are you expecting some quick wins?
- How will my performance be evaluated?
- Which issues preoccupy the staff; are these the same as the management?
- If you were me where would you focus your attention?
- What changes do you expect me to make?
- What are the most promising unexploited opportunities for growth?

- What would need to happen for the organisation to exploit the potential of these?
- Is the business really pursuing its stated vision and strategy?
- Why not? Is the strategy really taking it where it needs to go?
- What lurking surprises could detonate and push me off track?
- What are the most formidable barriers to making changes?
- What potentially damaging cultural or political missteps could I make?
- How is the job likely to change over the next couple of years?

2

Where appropriate, explore actual performance, morale, expectations, interaction, capability, systems, culture and reporting chains. The more you know, the more you can demonstrate your expertise.

Getting this information will help you to put together your First 100 days plan. Presenting this is an increasingly common part of the selection process and it is advisable to prepare a rough one for yourself even if you don't have to present it; so you have really thought through the impact you want to make in the early months.

- Where should I focus immediately?
- How am I being judged in the first three months and by what criteria?
- Whose expectations do I have to manage and what are they?

Talk about the money

The next stage hopefully, having convinced them that you are
the solution to all their problems, is to negotiate your offer. But
don't mention salary or your charge rates until they do. The
exception to this is when jobs are advertised without a fixed
salary level; 'competitive package will be paid'; here you might
want to double check pay scales when they call you up to invite
you to an interview. Even then, you are going to sell what you
can do for them so well that they should be prepared to break
the mould to get you on board. It doesn't matter what the
average is here: you are at the top of your game and they can't
afford to let you go to a more far-sighted competitor.

If the introduction is through a third party headhunter or
recruiter then a big part of their role is to manage negotiations.
Often their commission is based on a percentage of your salary
so theoretically they are on your side. Crazy though that is
because they should be negotiating on behalf of the party who
pays their bill. They will certainly get you a fair rate. There is a
surprising amount of leeway depending on your current or last
salary. For example, if you are on £34,000 they might offer you
£36,000, but if you are already on £38,000 then might offer you
£42,000, all for the same job. Changing jobs is an opportunity
to get a hefty uplift in salary, rather than relying on annual salary
increases. If you were underpaid in your last job compared to
your market worth you can still get round this with the great
phrase; 'Other opportunities which are being presented to me
are around £X.' You are not bragging about how much you
are worth. You are merely pointing out professionally what the
market says so they can go figure out your worth to them.

Happy endings

The illusionist Derren Brown has written about how we can
learn lessons from the Stoic philosophers on living a considered
life, called *Happy: Why More or Less Everything is Absolutely
Fine*. It's a great read and fits well with the rational emotional
behavioural coaching techniques I use in this book. He makes

the point that it is the end of the story we remember the most. The final chapter of a book *What Larks, Pip?* or the closing scenes of a film cloud our judgement of the entire tale. Think of *Bridget Jones's Diary*, *Slumdog Millionaire*, any Richard Curtis film, the end of *The Shawshank Redemption*; whatever they are, our favourite movies have powerful, evocative endings.

There's a lot in this book about initial impressions, but Brown demonstrates that how we feel at the end of meeting a candidate can really cloud our judgement. Make sure you manage the end of the meeting as carefully as the beginning. I'm not suggesting a quick song and dance routine, but a strong handshake, a thank you for their time and a confident exit, rather than stumbling out, grateful to escape. If you can, send the recruiter a bullet pointed summary of why you are interested in progressing, so they can summarise your considered feedback when they follow up.

Hopefully there will be good news and the next step is negotiating.

Salary and package negotiation tactics

Other people put the same price tag on you that you do yourself.

Negotiate! They expect you to, especially if this is part of your day job. Large corporates have compensation and benefits experts paid to negotiate with you. Never take the first offer without trying to up it somehow. They'll forget how much they paid you once the negotiations are over but it means a lot to you. Negotiate fairly and professionally. Good people – talent – know what they are worth. Ask yourself again; *'If I knew I was at the top of my game what would my expectations be now?'* You have looked like you were at the top of your game throughout this interview process and I hope you have also looked expensive and so they don't want to insult you with a low offer. I have avoided gender stereotyping so far in the book, but ladies, you know what I am saying I am sure. *'If you were a man in the same situation what would you do?'*

Don't mention money until they do. When they make their first offer say nothing. Pause for 30 seconds to look like you are reflecting. Most of us are braver doing this by phone rather than face to face. Wait until you get something in writing before you finally accept and pull the plug on other interview processes.

Hold your nerve. I have had clients who believe they were overpaid in their current job - some employers have a reputation for paying over the odds - so were prepared to take a drop if they had to. I'm pleased to say it hasn't happened yet. Employers do not expect you to take a cut when you change jobs; unless there is an obvious reason, such as moving into the charity sector or working locally. No one is going to the market to look for the cheapest employees; ok, maybe gang masters, but that's not relevant here. They want the best. If the role has different pay scales (e.g. £65,000 to £75,000) ask them what the different performance requirements are. What do they get from a £75,000 person that they don't get from a £65,000 person?

Don't be too grateful. If your confidence is low - perhaps if you are returning after a break - you might be prepared to compromise now and look for lower grade jobs or take a low offer. Once you are back at work and your confidence is returning you will kick yourself. Employers know this, so steer clear of hiring people who are selling themselves short anyway. Hold your nerve and get what you deserve. Ask yourself; *'If we were six months down the line and I knew I was doing great work, what would I expect to be paid?'* You know you are going to give them value for money, but you have to negotiate now.

Think about non-pay alternatives. When the opportunity to negotiate salary is limited, alternatives could be tax-deductible for them or not cost them anything, such as flexible hours, business class travel or paid professional development.

Define when your next salary review is. Get them to put this in your contract. You don't want to miss out on the annual salary increase because you joined in that year.

Negotiate professionally and don't play games. If you want the offer make sure they know that. You are going to work with these people so don't damage the relationship. Once you are happy with the offer accept it, subject of course to seeing it in writing, even running it past a lawyer if you want to. Now is the time to negotiate your non compete clauses also. Should you ring fence any customers or accounts you are bringing with you for example, so you can take them with you when you move on.

Should I take the job?

Your *Mind Flip* approach has worked and you have a job offer, perhaps more than one. This is quite often the case – when people are actively out on interview and if one company likes them, other companies will too. I sense that companies get competitive; they like to feel they are getting a candidate that other people are in the market for also.

Here's how to make a decision.

- Go back to your original goal. How closely does it match? If one offer exceeds your goal, go for that one.

- What is niggling you? In my experience, the little niggles you have now are the reasons you will regret taking the job offer in six months' time. In the same way, the niggles they have about you will be the reason they want to get rid of you in six months time. Remember when you dated someone and something annoyed you about them on the first date? Isn't that often the reason why you want to escape the relationship a year down the line?

- Don't ignore what you know deep down now, but you don't realize until you have been there for a few months. The long commute that you can only tolerate in the summer will be a killer in November. Don't be lured by other factors, if the basics aren't right for you.

- Don't worry if you can't do all the elements of the job description, or you are having a spell of impostor syndrome. That's normal. As long as you can do the key deliverables - and for goodness sake don't sign anything until you have nailed these down - then that's fine. They are hiring you and they think you can do the job, so leave it at that. If you have to, get some mentoring or training on your weaker areas before you start. No one is perfect, as long as you can do the areas where you will have the most impact that's fine. A challenge is good and your skills will develop to meet the challenges. Comfort zones are fine but you need to have more demands on your skillset over time. If you stay in a cosy job for too long, you will get bored and your performance levels will plateau and drop. It is time to move on.

- What are your fears? Are you frightened of success? Are you frightened of failure? With a coach or another good listener, get under the bonnet of what you are worried about and pinpoint what is really going on.

- Whose opinion counts? If your gut feeling is telling you to go for it, but you are unsure, are you looking at it through someone else's critical view? Who are you trying to please? Do they really matter?

- Get more data. Ask if you can go back into the business and meet the people you will be working for, or discuss targets, or spend a day in the office, clarify certain aspects of the role on the phone, etc. Don't get rushed into anything. Of course, there is a fine line between being perceived as precious and being appreciated as thorough; never procrastinate for too long.

- If you feel you can do better, you might want to hang on before committing. Obviously, if you have nothing else in the pipeline perhaps you should take it, but still keep an eye on the market, using the network you have built up during this job search process. It is much easier to get a job when you already have one.

- Don't leap 'from' something because a job appears to be better than the one you have now; it doesn't mean it is the right one for you. Often they are short-term moves. I see this when people have been in an organization for a long time. They aren't used to job seeking and maybe don't have much time. They take the first thing they are offered, realise they could do much better, move on to something else quite quickly and stay there for a long time. The first job they took turned out to be a stepping-stone to help them understand how good they were and gain confidence. Instead, leap 'to' something; not to get away from an unpleasant situation, but to something you actively want that gives you 80% of what you want, not 30%.

- I have seen all sorts of decision-making strategies, which often reflect the way people do their day job. Many people like to do SWOT analyses, while other people complete comparison spreadsheets. Of course, these are all subjective because they are only as good as the subconsciously biased information you put into them.

- Listen to the science of the gut. It's Monday morning, you've had a great weekend, which place do you want to go to work? If the people are nice and you believe in what you are doing, generally you will do well wherever you are. No amount of money or kudos will make up for that. Of course, it needs to be career enhancing in some way.

- Other people make a decision, sleep on it and see how they feel about their decision when they wake up in the morning. Flip a coin and notice what your gut tells you before you check which way it has landed. I know someone who wrote 'take it' and 'don't take it' on two bits of paper and watched which one her cat sat on. Least said about that the better!

- Remember you have time to make your decision between accepting a verbal offer and getting the paperwork. People expect you to have more than one choice and won't withdraw an offer if you don't say yes, immediately. You can tell how they will look after you by the way they manage your recruitment process and if they are unreasonably pressurising you, then include that in your decision-making about their suitability for you. However, once you know you want to work there and have negotiated your offer, remember they have egos too and tell them how delighted you are to be joining them.

- A client of mine said he was choosing between three excellent candidates for his job. He picked the one who made clear at interview that he wanted it. Employers want to know that if they will offer the job then, assuming some argy bargy while you agree terms, you will take the offer. It is embarrassing to offer to a candidate and have them turn down it down. No one likes rejection. So don't play too hard to get in the interview process, if you want to work there, say so.

Bear in mind that employers have fragile egos too. If you really want the job, don't play games, tell them.

How to resign with grace

Congratulations, you have a written job offer. If you are in a job, then of course you need to resign and here are several tips.

- Never burn your bridges. You need a reference. You may also need to go back there one day. That is a great coup for organisations; some even have talent scouts looking through LinkedIn for alumni. People leave; perhaps go to a competitor and then come back armed with fresh knowledge and experience; perhaps into a more senior role. It is a great 'the grass isn't really greener' message to the rest of the troops.

- Be clear on your restrictive covenants. If necessary, make sure your future employer is aware of these before you resign. This is particularly relevant for people who may be expected to bring business or clients with them. Are your performance expectations relying on this? Who will pay the legal fees if so? Better to have an upfront discussion and not proceed with a job offer, than to go ahead and get into legal hot water.

- Never resign if you are looking for a counter offer. Make sure you have thought through the opportunities in your current organisation, having a mature internal career conversation before you look externally. If you get a counter offer and stay, the psychological contract between you and your employer will be permanently damaged because the trust has gone. I've seen this so many times in the recruitment industry; when firms poach from each other constantly. People get an offer, get counter-offered, upset the people they should have joined and end up leaving six months later. They were then in a less strong position because their performance had dipped when they had their eye off the ball.

2

- Go into the meeting armed with your resignation in writing. Be professional; firm that you are leaving, but grateful for your time there. Make it clear that you will always be a great champion of the organisation. Once they know you are a good leaver, which doesn't reflect on their position or their management skills they will be more inclined to agree to your terms. Unless of course, they are a mad narcissist who takes everything personally when the conversation will be much more difficult. In this case, you have definitely made the right decision to move on. You will have to be much more tactical in a; 'It's not you, it's me' kind of way. They will interpret anything you say incorrectly and you need to get out of there as quickly as you can. I include this because there are so many of these out there, often in entrepreneurial start-ups. I often coach their seconds-in-commands on how to cope with them; either grow a very thick skin or move on.

- Offer to work your notice period; you legally have to do this anyway if you want to get paid. Often, they immediately insist on this, in the distress of losing a valuable employee. But once they realise they can cope without you and don't want you in the office, they will be more prepared to negotiate.

- Check your contract to see if you have the option of garden leave. Try and get a holiday in between jobs if you can to recharge your batteries. We don't often get opportunities for a break of more than a couple of weeks, so take it if you can.

2

This chapter will look at what might be going wrong if it's not happening: working through common problems people might experience; what the hunt saboteurs can do; and what happens when your values are not aligned with the work you do.

CHAPTER 14

It's not happening

When your job search is stalling, you must review what part of the process needs to be improved. Is your CV working? Are you getting first interviews but not second interviews? Do you always seem to get through to the end of the process but then don't get job offers? You might need some objective feedback; but you rarely get this from recruiters or from interviewers. They don't have time to explain, particularly if you are going to argue with them. Sometimes you get fobbed off with an excuse such as; *'you have too much experience'* which generally isn't true and can confuse matters. I know career coaches who prefer their clients not to ask for feedback because it is rarely honest. It's up to you and your relationship with the recruiter or interviewer.

Here are frequent problems, which I hope you are unlikely to experience unless you are working backwards through the book.

Why don't I get headhunted?
You are good at what you do but perhaps not visibly good. You might turn out results year after year and be a model employee. You hope someone is going to discover you and promote you, or find you a new role with a more appreciative boss. It rarely happens. Obviously you have to be good at what you do to

progress, although I am sure you have seen examples where people do well regardless; they get promoted out because that's the easiest way to get them out of your team. You also have to be seen to be good.

Shrinking violets are easy to overlook and don't demonstrate the necessary emotional intelligence needed to move up the corporate ladder. Understand what your personal brand is; your unique blend of expertise and articulate it, albeit with charm and humility. Be clear on what you have achieved and what you want to do next, both in your own organisation and externally. Put yourself up for promotions and opportunities. Make sure the recruiters in your sector know you. Become the talent that businesses want to recruit and retain.

I'm on LinkedIn; but it's not working for me

Check the first section to make sure your information is correct. This is where many people go wrong: they aren't working backwards from what a researcher would put in to find them. For example, you are an HR Director, your industry is the sector you work in – like financial services - not 'human resources' for example. Have you optimized your profile with the right skills and key words that a researcher would use to narrow down their search?

I can't even get a less senior role

Right now you're actively on the job market and not feeling too confident. You are applying for roles that are more junior than your current one. For example, you've been a Regional Sales Manager and now you are applying for a Territory role without people management responsibilities. It is very hard to go backwards. If you have other commitments and passions you want to focus on now, explain that. Otherwise, the recruiter will assume that once you have your mojo back you'll be off again, leaving them with an angry client. They are paid to find candidates who are on their way up in their career; organisations have plenty of their staff who are plateauing, they don't pay fees for more of the same. Create a career narrative that demonstrates why they should recruit you and why their role meets your objectives at this stage of your career.

No one is responding to my CV

That's because it is full of tedious hyperbole. Recruiters look first at the most recent job on your CV: the company and job title. If they are interested, they read on to find evidence of success. This needs to be measured through Key Performance Indicators achieved, percentage improvements, how the business was when you left compared to when you started, etc. They want tangible evidence that you are the best at what you do. Generally the best indicator of future success is what you have done in the past, in a relevant context. Recruiters want to see facts.

Your personal statement should summarise what you have done in the past, what you want to do next and the competencies that bridge the two. The rest of the document is supporting evidence.

My networking isn't getting results

Judging by most of my outplacement client experiences, most roles still come from your own network, particularly at senior level. Actually, your network's network; one step removed from you. The more you have nurtured your network on the way up, the more people are happy to do you favours and make introductions for you. Opportunities tend to be created because people know you are good, you clearly articulate what you do well and because you are the right culture fit; people trust you and share your values. Within your network I count previous colleagues and managers, direct and indirect reports, customers, suppliers (lawyers, auditors), mentors, anyone who has a vested interest in getting you back to work, as well as all the external relationships you have accumulated. Your contacts need to understand what you do now and what you want to do next; are you explaining this well enough?

2

It's very slow out there

It might well be, but are you sure you are doing enough activity? You have to do double the amount you think necessary. People who find work more quickly than other people put more effort into the early stages of their search. They create opportunities for themselves, through networking, talking to recruiters, applying for roles, making direct approaches, working on their LinkedIn profile, using job boards judiciously, attending events and being generally active in their market and they know what's going on. They continuously refine their marketing message and get it out there. They aren't wasting time on job alerts.

They treat this as a 'mystery shopper' opportunity, talking to several organisations to find the best fit and learning best practice on the way. They realize they need to have several irons in the fire to land the right job; probably more than they first think. They also welcome rejection because they understand that statistically these bring them closer to an offer; although they sometimes need extra support with this aspect. Contemporary recruitment processes are long drawn out; internal candidates can sneak onto the short-list and briefs change. Successful job seekers need to stay resilient and focused. This attitude is in itself appealing to hiring organisations because it reflects their general approach to business.

Those job boards are rubbish

Have you used the filters correctly? You need to be specific in the boxes you tick, not leave them open so you come up on all searches. Researchers want the smallest but highest quality sample, not thousands of CVs. Again, think of the criteria someone would need to put in to find you and get those key words right. If you aren't getting accurate job alerts and calls it means your key words are incorrect.

Choose one or two well-established job boards as a trial and also smaller ones that specifically focus on your function or industry or location. Try them, if they don't work you can always take down your CV. Firms search for recent applications; refresh your CV regularly by tweaking it slightly and reloading it.

Don't send off hasty applications. Read the small print, make sure you have evidence of successfully fulfilling the main responsibilities of the role and send off an application that is thorough and spelt correctly. You would be horrified at the rubbish companies receive. For example, there are thousands of 'mangers' on LinkedIn and I am sure many of them say they have a 'keen eye for detail.' Use the job boards for research: who is recruiting where, what the common requirements are, which organisations are active in which sector/space and so on.

2

There aren't any jobs out there that I want to apply for

You should be networking to create opportunities for yourself. Applying for jobs is part of the Smart Job Search Process at the start of the book, revisit Chapter 2: It's Not About You. You want to keep your options open. It's also interesting to see the response you get and can be a good confidence boost.

However, advertised jobs do not reflect the real job market. The received wisdom is that only about 20% of jobs are advertised these days. Of course, these vary from sector to sector and at different levels. The public sector advertises all their jobs. However, many organisations have stopped. They don't want to be swamped with applicants. Even recruitment consultants don't advertise all their roles. Some might be confidential, or they might want to get on the phone and generate their own candidates instead of relying on active job seekers. Headhunters are paid to do that. Pick up the phone and talk to them about your experience; some have relationships with their clients to send them good talented candidates with particular skillsets in particular locations. Don't assume they don't want you because they aren't advertising for you.

Hunt saboteurs

Never give up. Go back to the Smart Job Search Process at the start of the book and work out where the gaps are. If you aren't getting anywhere is there a possibility you could be sabotaging your own search? For example, when I have a client who should be getting work but for some reason isn't, that can be a clue that deep down they want to do something different. Perhaps you need to explore other options.

Your values; golden handcuffs?

Think about your values. These are your GPS navigation guides for your career. If they aren't aligned, then they won't take you where you want to go in the long-term. When people aren't content at work, or they aren't wholeheartedly pursuing a job search, it can be a clue that their values aren't reflected in their choices.

Do your personal values match those of the work you do, the people you work with or the organization your work for? What are the most important things to you in the way you work and live? Does your work – or the type of work you are looking for – reflect those values? Your values should determine your priorities and your career choices. Values are often described as 'running through you like words in a stick of seaside rock candy' they are an integral part of you.

Here are several value prompts, to guide you in identifying what is most important to you at this stage of your career.

Achievement, aesthetically pleasing work environment, attractiveness, commitment, compassion, creativity, dependability, determination, empathy, equality, faith, family, financial rewards, freedom, generosity, giving back, goodness, healthy living, humour, integrity, intelligence, justice, joy, love, loyalty, money, motivation, originality, open-mindedness, professionalism, positivity, resilience, reliability, selflessness, social status, spirituality, thoughtfulness, tolerance, travel opportunity, understanding, vitality and warmth.

Note whether your values are intrinsic and have their own reward (creativity, freedom, intellectual challenge) or extrinsic, which usually have worth attached to them by other people (social status or financial rewards.) Most of us have a mixture of the two and these may change over time. The extrinsic values can sometimes handcuff us to unhappy career choices; or other people's choices for us rather than our own. Check your assumptions – how do you know you wouldn't achieve the financial results you need - if you made a career change that reflected your values? Remember most career changes happen incrementally rather than drastically and you can take a slightly winding route to get to where you want to end up.

2

PART
3

JUST FOR YOU

This chapter will help you win the work you want and negotiate the best rates for your skills and the value you provide.

CHAPTER 15

Self-employed; Freelancers; Contractors; Consultants; and Interims; Be your own boss

Make a launch for freedom

You've decided to follow your entrepreneurial leanings and take a leap of faith by working for yourself. Good for you. You are passionate about what you do and confident you can support yourself. Often the next course of action is to build a website explaining everything you do and then promote all this on social media. Wrong. You know what I am going to say next. It's the first rule of sales and this book. It's not about you. It's about them and their problem.

Start with the mind of your potential client and work backwards from there. Walk in their shoes for a while. What are their problems? What keeps them awake at night? Find organisations who have used freelancers and contractors like you before. Why did they use them? What were the problems they wanted the freelancer to solve and what results did they expect from them? How did they measure those results?

3

Once you understand the problem you are solving, you can write your website and your marketing collateral with your target clients in mind. It's the same process for you as for finding any other kind of work: full time employment, part-time or portfolio. You create your own opportunities by understanding the problems you solve and finding organisations with those problems. Clients don't come to you (unless you have a massive budget to spend on search engines). You can't simply be good at what you do; you have to be good at your marketing strategy too.

One of the greatest challenges when working for yourself is how to charge for your time. You have to factor in all your costs of working. Driving a cab for Uber gives you an hourly rate but it isn't until you factor in all your other costs (finance, insurance, administration) that you know how much profit you really make. There is a danger that you end up overworked and worse off financially than you were when you were a wage slave (with paid holidays, sickness and pension contributions).

Charge for your time; what is it worth?

By this I mean what is your time worth to you and worth to the person paying for it? Working out daily rates for contract or interim assignments isn't difficult. Often organisations have fixed charge rates of the job, or your recruiter can advise you.

The formula many agencies use is to add your benefits to your annual salary and divide this amount by 220. This final figure is your minimum daily rate. This is based on the assumption that interims work 220 days a year, allowing for down time between assignments, holidays and weekends. You need to charge a bit on top to factor in holiday and sick pay, pension contributions, insurances and employer's national insurance contributions.

Career interims are normally paid through their own limited company or via an umbrella company. It's not uncommon for interims to charge double or even treble the hourly rate of an employee but this is turnover, not profit. You aren't being greedy, but allowing for all the extras that employees take for granted. Employers get the benefit of your skillset at no risk to them: they aren't committing to hiring you. Often consulting is an extended probation period for potential hires. It is an ideal way to position yourself as the internal candidate when a permanent role comes up, if you want to return to permanent employment.

Charge on value; not hours

The greater challenge comes when you are freelance and creating an opportunity from scratch, perhaps for one off projects. How do you price these? You first need to be completely clear on what you deliver and have real pride in what you do. If you don't value yourself, you can never sell the value of what you do.

A common mistake made by rookie consultants and freelancers, grateful for the work, is to focus on input (billable hours, hourly rates, hours of work) rather than output (what is my contribution to the organization, how will they make money or save money from having me there, what is my contribution to their business goals and strategy?). This gets you off the fee issue and on to the value of what you do.

'Your charge rates depend on the perceived value of your services. Clients pay for value, not hours.'

Alan Weiss, Value-Based Fees, 2002

3

It is crucial to establish value with your client if you want to maximize your income. That value can then be charged as a flat fee/retainer rather than based on the hours you work. This way you can manage several retainers at once and increase your earnings. It's obviously the results and benefits you create that make the difference, the value isn't from you turning up and feeling under pressure to look busy.

People believe they get what they pay for, so position yourself as the McKinsey/Tesla of your sector. You want to create a vibe of 'if you are serious about wanting to change or do this, talk to me, otherwise don't waste my time'. It takes guts to hold your nerves like this, but you want serious clients who are committed to the project you are going to do and will back you to do it. Committed also means establishing outputs and timeframes and getting buy-in from other people in the business. All of this helps you to do a better job and means you will throw the kitchen sink at delivering for them. You aren't going to fail are you? Have the confidence to charge accordingly. It comes down to our previous question: *'If I was at the top of my game what would I do now?'*

A hard lesson I learnt when I started my own freelance career is that being busy and booked up isn't always the smart option. It is easy to be overworked and underpaid when you are selling your time. Tempting though it is to say yes, to what comes your way, there are only so many hours in the week. You have to ask yourself; *'If I am doing this with my time what am I not doing?'* Factor in time for prospecting for new business to build your pipeline, doing administration and necessary, relaxing down time too. Something is not always better than nothing if the rate is too low. It can be hard to let go of unprofitable business, but it is the only option if you want to earn a good living.

Another lesson I learnt is that equal to value in negotiating fees is integrity. I will guarantee an immediate, no quibble, refund of my coaching fees if the client can put in writing their reasons for cancelling our contract. It gives my clients a reassurance but also means that I choose my clients carefully. If I don't think they will get the results they want, I won't work with them. It's a two-way benefit and means I set careful contracts and fortunately I haven't ever had to return a fee.

My clients who have opted for a freelance career often get several regular projects, which gives them a reliable income and forms the core of their working week. This work can come from their last employer; reluctant to let them go, they are happy to maintain the relationship and retain them to work on vital projects. They'll be able to get a fair rate for the work and charge a premium for other work to fit around them. Once they understand they need to add marketing, sales and consulting skills to their existing skillset, they build sustainable careers. I doubt they get much more time to relax, but the freedom and control they have over their work is priceless to them.

3

CHAPTER 16

Graduates: how to find work and get in the door

All the principles in this book apply equally to you, as a new entrant to the workplace as much as to someone who is many years ahead of you. Remember, it's definitely not about you. It's about how you stand out from your peers based on what you can do for a potential employer. That can be hard to explain if you are up against other graduates who are chasing the same jobs as you, all with limited relevant experience.

Start with a reality check

First of all, when an employer is hiring a graduate all they are really getting is potential. Someone with the level of education they want and the right attitude. This means someone who wants to do the job well, will work harder than everyone else and will fit into the culture. Someone who will ask for help when they don't know what to do, can communicate on paper and

3

in person and has a positive frame of mind. A positive frame of mind is a curious nature, an optimistic approach to solving problems and a grown-up attitude to work. This includes, turning up on time fit for work, dressing appropriately, keeping your phone switched off during the day, managing your moods, and behaving like a professional.

To get short-listed for interview you have to demonstrate that you have the right attitude and frame of mind. This can be shown in the enthusiastic, focused way you apply to them and also in any work experience or achievements you can demonstrate on your CV. You can't simply say you are an 'enthusiastic hard worker' if you don't have evidence of hard work on your CV to back up your claim.

Blag work experience

Get as much work experience as you can, whether paid or not, as soon as you are old enough, through all your holidays. This is the best way of differentiating yourself. It shows you are genuinely interested in the field you have done your research, understand the issues and are serious.

I whole-heartedly dislike those internships that middle-class kids get through their parents' networks; *'Mummy rang up Emma, who does her PR and she got me a week working with her, I had sooo... much fun.'* I disliked them until I needed to do the same for my own children of course, when I admit I swallowed my principles and called in favours. If you can't beat them etc.

Get yourself experience where ever you can and never be afraid to ask for help. Most people are keen to help enthusiastic young people get a leg-up. Develop a thick skin. Getting work is always a numbers game so expect some rejection.

Make a smart CV and send several well-crafted personalised emails to the heads of whatever company or department you want to work for and ask if you can come in for a week or more.

It makes such a difference when you get the email address for the person you want to work for rather than going through HR. No out-dated; 'Sir or Madam' emails please. Senior people have egos, so stroke them. You can make a powerful mentor for life and actually have nothing to lose. A personal email makes it harder to ignore, whereas sending one to HR or through formal channels on the website - although you may want to do that also - can more easily be rejected.

Write something snappy, which catches their eye without being time consuming and explains what you can do for them. You don't have to say what a clever, enthusiastic and passionate little cookie you are. You are demonstrating this in your approach to them.

Dear Mrs Smith

I read the article about you in this week's Sunday Times. I was so inspired by what you have achieved.

I am also from Croydon, am in Year 12 at John Halstead School and hoping to study Economics at University. I am looking for summer work experience within financial services in the week of 29 June onwards as this is my chosen field. I know you must get lots of requests like these but I would be so grateful if I could come and work with you. My CV is attached, detailing my IT skills and my contact details are below.

Thank you so much for your help.

Kyle Denis

3

Or

Dear Mr Purdy

I am starting a Foundation Degree in Art & Design at Swallowsborn College in September and I am looking for work experience during the summer. I have been a fan of your books since my parents bought me The World's Best Trucks when I was a toddler and I have been collecting them ever since.

I would like to be an Illustrator (I know that's how you started) and would be so grateful if I could do some work with you from 1 July onwards. I'm happy to do anything to pull my weight and attach my CV and some of my designs so you can see my work. I also speak fluent Spanish, which may be useful as I know you translate your titles into Spanish also.

My mobile number is 0999 090900 and I would be keen to have a chat with you or one of your team about how I can contribute to more great Purdy Books.

Kind regards
Ashton Krawler

Never be shy about this. Most people who work complain that they are short-staffed, over-worked, their colleagues don't pull their weight, their staff don't have enough initiative or they simply can't find enough good people. In short, you could be a valuable member of staff and they will be delighted to hear from you. It's a numbers game though so don't put all your eggs in one basket. Or bastard, to quote Dorothy Parker.

Work with what you've got, don't worry about what you haven't

You are now looking for a permanent job and don't have much relevant work experience for your CV? Try and get some of course, but if you are making applications now, then do the best with what you've got. Find anything that shows the type of person you are, your character and passions and write it up compellingly. Here's how to explain some less than relevant work experience.

For a job in marketing consumer goods

'I worked at Sainsburys in Wood Green from my last year at school and in all my university holidays, on the cash register and on the shop-floor. As well as the discipline and team-work skills that come from this type of work, it gave me grass-roots experience in consumer spending patterns because I had to restock the shelves for the brands that sold out first. I learned the products that sold best to which type of customer, where they were displayed in the store and I observed when and how the customers shopped.'

Ok, this is stretching your shelf-stacking a bit, but again you have little to lose and it shows chutzpah if nothing else. It also shows you have a great work ethic, will commit to jobs, will stick at them and not give up. Illustrating that you have worked, while other people have been partying, has got to be a good thing.

3

If all you've got is babysitting, then show the skills you've used

'I did heavy essay topics for my 'A' levels and my school said they would prefer it if students with this work load didn't do part-time work. However, I was saving up to go travelling in the summer holidays so got round the 'work' ban by doing baby-sitting as often as I could. I regularly picked up two young girls from primary school, took them home on the bus, cooked them a fairly healthy tea and supervised their homework until their

parents got home in the early evening. One child was entering a drama competition and I wrote a script for her to perform.'

It's much more effective to illustrate your skills like this, than to say you are hard-working, responsible, work on your own initiative, etc. We can all say that. You need data to prove it.

You will find something to write about, even if it's personal
'I live with my mother and my younger brother. My mother works shifts in the City, returning home about 9pm most evenings, so from the age of 14 I collected my brother from school, cooked dinner for us, perhaps took him to a sports club and did basic chores around the house. My mother doesn't speak English, so I also translated all the letters and bills that come to the house and helped her as much as I could.'

You might not think it sounds like much, but this kind of detail tells us so much about your character. A client of mine said he hired on how far people had come, based on their own efforts, so she always wanted to know their starting point. If employers are screening out on expensive extra-curricular hobbies then that's their loss. Plenty more will want you because of who you are. Be honest and never neglect this kind of information. It shows reliability, guts, commitment, dedication, loyalty and responsibility. Be proud and shout about it.

Get your head around what the employer is looking for
You might feel like you are still a student when you are going to interviews, but your employer is going to evaluate you as a Marketing Assistant, Trainee Lawyer, Associate Mental Health Worker or whatever the job is you are for. They are comparing you to people already in the business, probably their best hires of the past, rather than against your student cohort. Trained interviewers may be better at fair comparisons, but at some stage you will meet potential managers or team members who all compare you to themselves. They will measure your answers

against the answers they would give themselves now, not always taking into account your lack of experience. That's life. Step up. Do your research and walk the talk.

When you look and behave like the person you want to be, you will become that person

Turn up looking like you are already doing the job. If you have to, visit the company a few days before the interview, hover around outside and see what the employees look like and then turn up looking like they do, on a very good day. Now is the time to conform, change your culture when you are in there. Go shopping if you need to, to buy the 'look'. You can buy a cheap high street version and trade up when you can afford to. It's as much as looking like you have made an effort as anything else.

Come prepared, with notes, questions to ask, in a smart bag or folder. Behave like you are doing the job already. You wouldn't turn up for a meeting without a pen and paper so arm yourself for an interview.

It is not cool to be cool when job seeking

Employers are hiring brains and potential. I have taken part in plenty of graduate interviews and been amazed at the sloppy, horizontal way some people present themselves. I avoid clichéd, negative, millennial stereotyping because in my experience the younger generation often have an amazing work ethic and far better discipline than I did at that age. However, not all millennials have got the message. They appear blasé, not looking smart enough, not having done their research about the organisation, not preparing answers to obvious questions and generally not giving the impression they want it badly enough. They may be the 'best' on paper, but employers will always go for the candidate who wants it the most and demonstrates the most mature work ethic. Why would they waste time training you, if you are going to change your mind about working there and leave?

3

Often these ill-prepared candidates are merely hiding their vulnerability with an unhelpful defence mechanism. If they gave it 100% (as they say to the judging panel on those TV shows) they risk a dent to their self-esteem when they get rejected.

They subconsciously sabotage their chances of being hired by giving themselves the excuse of; *'I didn't have time to prepare properly so they turned me down'*; or *'I was still hung over, so they didn't think I was enthusiastic enough.'* Stick your neck out and go for it. If you are nervous and you think it shows, then you can say; *'this is my first interview and I am feeling nervous. Can you repeat that question please?'* Where's the shame in that? You may get brownie points for self-awareness and honesty.

You may be rejected – in fact it is likely that you will - given the number of people going for every job. But you'll learn from it and keep improving your performance. Statistically it is highly unlikely you will be offered every job you apply for. There is no shame in getting turned down for a job, but you owe it to yourself to give it your best shot.

You're hired; how to cope with your first job and beyond

Now you have a job, whether permanent or work experience, it goes without saying you have to build on the experience as much as you can and make the most of it. Below are eleven strategies for keeping your job and getting up the next rung of the ladder.

Here's what they'd like to tell you at Induction but either assume you know already or they don't want to be patronising. It's not going to stop me from spelling them out! These are strategies for navigating the work place and building your brand, both internally and externally. There are more throughout the book, such as building a strong LinkedIn profile, as necessary for internal networking as job seeking later on and learning networking techniques. This list is for people new to the work place who are finding their feet. And their pigeonhole!

1. Stick at it
Once you have a permanent job, you ideally need to stay in it for no less than one year, but preferably a minimum of two or three years. That's usually how long it takes for you to become a productive and profitable employee. There is a myth that you need to 'move on' but if you are learning and developing your skills in an organisation and are happy there than there is absolutely no need to change jobs. Just because you are on the headhunters' radar doesn't mean you have to jump ship. Soak up as much experience and training as you can, your first job sets the standard for the work to come.

2. Work is called work for a reason
A good work ethic means turning up early and sometimes staying beyond your contracted hours, so you can do a good job and shine. There is no merit in working long hours for presenteeism – that just leads to burn out. However, sometimes you need to go the extra mile and if you want a job that challenges you then you won't be able to watch the clock.

3. Put your hand up and ask for more
When you can take on more than your job description and start performing to the level above you, taking on extra work, mentoring newer employees and training the new batch of work experience people, then you will discover the trick to getting promoted! Never wait to be asked. Just do it. Always look and behave like the job you want to do next. Learn to glide a bit – you know the expression of seeming like a swan on the surface and paddling furiously underneath? Some people seem to think that it is career-enhancing to huff and puff round the office, moaning about how much work they have to do. The opposite is true – try and give off the vibe of being in control - with capacity for more.

3

The flip side of this is learning to put your hand up to get help. People want to help other people. Your success reflects on your manager. They also want to nip problems in the bud. I've heard managers complain about younger employees who are so used to solving problems online (forums, groups, YouTube) that they have stopped asking for help, or never learnt to. Consequently, small issues can escalate. If you aren't sure about something, ask for clarification. Try not to get overwhelmed either: if you can't find a coping strategy yourself ask for help, from colleagues first and from your managers. It is likely they will have faced the same issues already and can tell you what worked for them.

4. Get a mentor

The most effective people I have met at work have naturally developed informal mentoring relationships with more senior people. This is often your first boss, or your boss's boss, a senior person who is minded to help people in their career, recommending them when necessary and guiding them about the way things are done. If someone offers you advice and help, take it gratefully and follow up with them on your progress. It's a two-way relationship, they will look good on the back of your success and besides that, they will get satisfaction from supporting you.

6. Add value

When I interviewed candidates as a recruiter, I always wanted to know what they could do over and above their job descriptions. Think of several initiatives you can take to improve the business, either for the staff or externally, for the clients or customers, and do it. For example, that's how my GP's surgery has a fantastic wildlife garden for patients to work in, to improve their wellbeing. Other people organise the soft-ball league at their company, or the monthly quiz nights, or organise the leaving collections for colleagues. Large companies have Corporate Social Responsibility departments doing charitable projects you can get involved in, albeit sometimes for taxation and PR benefits, but the personal benefits of participation are enormous. Get involved and do more.

7. Think for yourself

Learn the ropes but never be frightened to politely, challenge the status quo, once you have passed probation. Ask yourself; *'Why are we doing this'* and *'Is this the best way to achieve this outcome'*. If you can find a better way, pilot it, experiment and tactfully present it. I've never come across an organisation that doesn't want its staff to come up with innovative and new ways to improve what it does.

8. Manage your time

> *'Doing something unimportant well*
> *does not make it important'*
>
> Tim Ferris

It is so easy to be busy fools at work, faffing around responding to emails and wasting time on waffly meetings. Know what your priorities are at work, what you will be measured on and where you have the most impact. If you don't know this, sit down with your manager and agree it (go in to the meeting with a plan and a draft or updated job description). Make sure you do the most important tasks that will enhance your career and give you the most visibility. Drop the irrelevant tasks you do or delegate them as soon as you are able to – that's how you start your own management career - by creating work for someone else to do. You don't get points these days for being a hero/victim/easy-touch. You get them for performing tasks that make a difference, solving problems and having maximum impact. Plan your time around these and always know where your time goes.

3

9. Build your resilience

The modern workplace is tough and learning to bounce back is a crucial skill. You will make mistakes; that's how all of us learn. Everyone has bad days. Never beat yourself up. Learn from it and move on and do not make the same mistake again.

Practise cognitive reframing to rationally appraise the situation, acknowledge how you are feeling and then take action to move forward. It's all about perception. It is how you perceive a challenge that is important, rather than the challenge itself. Is it something you have the tools and skills to cope with? Compare the following reactions to the same situation.

Reaction A: magnifies our weaknesses and 'awfulizes' the situation.

The project is going over budget and I don't think my manager likes me. She never talks to me and just gets on with her own work. It is a disaster. I am rubbish at this job and will never survive here. I knew I was biting off more than I could chew. I am heading off to the pub now and should probably resign before they put me on a warning.

Reaction B: which is a more evidence-based approach, allows you to take strategies to move forward.

The project is going over budget but if I sit down with the delivery team I think we can work out ways to claw back our margin by cutting costs on transport and production. Also, I need to sit down with my managers to get their input. They have been so busy on other work that I haven't had any feedback. They must have been in this situation before so will have ideas about how to deal with the client. I am tired and feeling under pressure but if this comes off it will be a real coup. I'll write out a to-do list before I leave today and get an early night.

10. Know your strengths

> 'Strong people always have strong weaknesses too.
> Where there are peaks, there are valleys.
> And no one is strong in many areas.
> Measured against the universe of human knowledge,
> experience and abilities, even the greatest genius would
> have to be rated a total failure.
> There is no such thing as a 'good man'.
> Good for what? is the question.'

Peter Drucker, founder of modern management

Acknowledge you have strengths as well as development areas.
You are only human! Development areas are what your HR
department will call your weaknesses. Apart from the perils of
aiming to be perfect, realise that it is impossible to be brilliant at
everything.

Some of us are great at negotiating, but not so good at the
follow-up correspondence confirming the deal. Many sales
people are good at cold calling for new business, but less
confident at building long-term client relationships. Several
people hate public speaking, but are excellent in smaller
meetings; other people can do big-picture strategy, but dislike
routine administration. I get lots of work, but struggle to send
out an invoice without a typo, even with my glasses on!

Play to your strengths and focus on developing them. Build a
reputation for excellence in the areas that count. Work on your
weaknesses so you are good enough to get by at these tasks
and if possible, avoid them, delegating them as soon as you can
afford to.

Remember successful careers are about differentiating yourself
by solving specific problems, not being average at everything.
Which problems do they need you to solve? Don't hedge

3

your bets and be homogenous, vanilla, all things to all men. Take a risk at being exceptional in one or two areas and make a name for yourself. Choose your own pigeonhole, your area of expertise. This will become your personal brand and what people will remember about you.

11. Learn soft skills, particularly how to be assertive

It's hard to avoid difficult conversations at work and the sooner you learn to communicate maturely the better. Learn to see things from other people's perspectives. Avoid making issues personal, keep your points specific and factual and be clear on what you want to happen instead. Never get shouty when under pressure, that's the way they behave in soap operas, not at work. Be professional and calm. You will find that generally other people will mirror your behaviour. If someone shouts at you, walk away until they calm down. Here are examples of win-win conversations.

Avoid: Your department is disorganised, you dump work on us on a Friday evening and expect us to stay late to finish it. It's unreasonable.

Say: When you bring work to us on a Friday evening we assume you expect us to complete it before we finish for the weekend. It would be really helpful if you gave it to us by lunchtime on Friday, or put a note on the files that you don't need them done until Monday.

Avoid: I am not attending any more meetings, they are a complete waste of my time.

Say: When I sit in on the planning meetings, I find a lot of the agenda isn't really relevant to me. For the next couple of meetings I will trial getting a copy of the minutes and see if that is enough information.

Avoid: You are a rubbish manager, always breathing down my neck. It stresses me out.

Say: When you give me a new project, let's agree the deliverables and milestones up front, so I can get on with the work and you feel more comfortable leaving me to it because we have set dates in the diary to catch up.

11. Learn to manage upwards

Be a good citizen and think about what is causing stress for your managers and colleagues. Put yourself in their shoes, they might be working parents, have ill relatives, be under pressure from their managers or have health issues. Or they might be tired! Who knows what is going on with them, or what they have to cope with before and after they get to work? Never assume it is about you if they are in less than good form. Many managers are less skilled than we would like them to be, so learn tactics to manage up and get the best out of them.

For example, communicate sensitively, by saying, *'I know you have a lot to do with a model client this morning, can we catch up for five minutes later in the day to discuss my client, say 2 pm, how does that suit you?'* This is much nicer than an unscheduled interruption or demand.

3

Be pleasant. They say that honey catches more flies than vinegar. Say thank you when you get help, in the way you'd like some appreciation and feedback coming your way in return. Manage your moods too, get enough sleep, eat healthily and factor in regular exercise sessions. Getting these basics right will help you to cope when working life gets more demanding. If you are feeling weak and tired, you might not have the resources to develop your skills, manage difficult people or think of a strategy to get round a new problem.

Ask for feedback, not in any annoying, needy way, but in a development focused and specific way. For example, saying; *'Do you think I should have negotiated a bit earlier in that meeting?'* This is more helpful information to everyone than saying; *'Was I ok in that meeting?'*

Exercise: Future proofing your success

Once you are in your new job, you have passed your probation and you are seeing how the land lies, take time to think about the question below, taken from 'The 99 Essential Business Questions'; Campari, Glassman et al. Record your answer and make a plan for making your answer happen.

- Looking back from three years into the future, what three things did I do to achieve the success I had planned?

3

This chapter is for mums and people returning to work after a break. It will show you how to: handle the baby or the elephant in the room; and talk about your gap with confidence; rather than apologising for it.

CHAPTER 17

Returners, Mums and Carers; never mind the gap

3

Return to work after a break

The technique of focusing on your skills and the solutions you provide rather than selling your own brilliance has really helped my mum returner clients and other people returning to work after any kind of break, self-imposed or otherwise. You may be asked what you have done while out of the work place, but never assume the recruiter is disapproving. They are simply asking, possibly testing your resilience and ability to cope with the pressure. Or they might be jealous that you have taken a break and they haven't been able to. Who knows, but never make assumptions.

If you feel it is 'wrong' to have taken time out of work then spend some time working out why you feel that way. Whose definition of a 'good' career are we working to here? Not the academic one as defined by John Arnold, Work Psychology, 2005, *'the sequence of employment-related positions, roles, activities and experiences encountered by a person.'*

The sequence element is reassuring. But it can also be periods in and out of work or returning to study. We certainly aren't talking about a job for life anymore. So never apologise for taking time out, for whatever reason.

The trick for returners, as ever, is to flip the conversation from talking about you, to how you are keen to use your SAP skills, quantitative research experience, advanced Mandarin or love of animals, whatever is it. Your confidence will quickly come back. But remember to do the usual tricks while you are waiting for it to catch up with your need/desire to return to paid employment. Buy the smartest clothes you can afford; get a good haircut; do whatever you feel is going to make you appear more confident. Fake it to make it here: if you appear more confident, you will look more confident. Hide your vulnerability under your armour and always look like you not only fit in to the company you want to work for, but you are almost the next level up.

Stay current in your break if at all possible. Keep up to date with changes in your industry and perhaps pick the brains of previous colleagues before you return. Keep an eye on LinkedIn to keep in touch.

Update your CV
Taking a break from work can make your confidence plummet, or it can re-energise you. The problem is more about your perception of your time out, than the time out itself. You've taken a break? Big deal. Never hide it, turn it into a selling point. For example, your personal statement can look like this.

Having taken voluntary redundancy from Gamble & Co, I decided to take a career break. During this time, I've supported my wife in her embryonic eduTech business using my financial modelling skills to develop her business plan and secure her first contracts. Now the business is off the ground, it's time for me to return to corporate life, with new entrepreneurial experience to add to my financial management skillset.

Or

After I completed the £770 million systems integration project at Axon, I decided it was an ideal time to take a career break and fulfil my long held ambition of travelling across Southern Africa. It's been amazing and the highlight was building houses for a non-profit charity in Lesotho. But I am now ready to return to the comforts of the business world, using my knowledge of complex transformation and integration projects and adding greater cross-cultural understanding.

These are merely suggested styles to help you explain the gap confidently. If you have done voluntary work in your gap that is relevant to what you want to do next, you can put this at the top of your career history on the CV. This might give you the transferable skills you need to move into another sector.

3

Questions to expect and those to reject
These are fairly standard 'returners' interview questions you should prepare for.
- How have you kept up to date with what is going on in our industry?
- What challenges do you think we are facing in our sector at the moment?
- What recent new stories have you read about in the sector?

- How have you changed in your period out of employment?
- How do you know your skills are up to date?
- What are your strengths and development areas?

Ensure you have really good examples of how you have successfully filled the main criteria of the role in the past. Avoid mentioning the date of your achievements when you are talking them through, instead tell them the name of the organisation where you did the work. No 'back in the day' stuff, which draws attention to how long ago it was.

Sell yourself as someone who can hit the ground running, even if you are feeling a bit wobbly on the inside. You want the interviewer to have confidence in you.

Do you mention the baby, or elephant, in the room?

If you are a mum changing jobs or returning to work, should you mention your children at interview? Legally, they shouldn't ask you and you don't need to mention it. The reality of course, is that they are wondering what your circumstances are. It is naïve to think this isn't a factor in their decision-making. I realise that dads also take parental leave, but of course they don't actually get pregnant so they never face the discrimination some women do.

Interviews should only be about your ability to do the job. Your personal circumstances should not be on the agenda. However, in the real world, interviewers probe, with varying degrees of subtlety as the table below demonstrates.

Interview questions to expect	What they are trying to find out
Are you available to work overtime?	Have you got kids?
What are your long-term career plans?	When are you planning in having your next baby and will you come back to work afterwards?
What hours are you available to work and can you stay late at short notice?	Have you got good childcare and how many kids have you got anyway?
Are your qualifications and references under any other name?	Are you married or a single parent? If we have your married name as well then we can do a social media search to check you out.
This job can be quite stressful. As an organisation we make great efforts to support our employees' wellbeing but it is important that you also make efforts to cope. What strategies have you got in place for that?	Does your partner have a big job also or can they be relied on to pick up the slack when you need to work late? What emergency childcare have you got in place if your children are ill and can't go to school because we'll need you to turn up? Where does your mother live?
What motivates you?	Have you got a rich husband? Do you need the money badly enough to put up with all the crap that will be coming your way?

3

Here are three options for how to deal with these questions during the interview process.

1. You don't have to mention your family life. It is not uncommon for women of a certain age to remove wedding or engagement rings at interviews.

2. You can discuss it in the first interview yourself and nip any issues in the bud yourself with a brilliant answer.

   I've loved being at home with my children, but now they are at school I am itching to get back to full time employment. It's my time now and we need a second salary coming in too. Kids are demanding these days. My lot are really ungrateful about me being at home with them. They only want me working again to pay for their phone upgrade.

   Or

   I feel this is the right time in my career to put myself forward for promotion. My family is complete now and I am ready to make a full commitment again to my career and frankly the overseas business travel will actually give me a sneaky break from the daily grind. My partner works for himself so he is around to pick up the slack.

   Or

   My boyfriend and I have bought our first house. We've taken on a huge mortgage and I've decided to commit the next ten years to building my career and earning as much as I can before we even think about starting a family.

3. You take the honest approach. Explain you have children and you are fully able to cope with the demands of the role, but hope that they will be reasonably flexible to accept occasional working from home, trunked up hours or whatever

you need to do. Make sure you have made them realise they can't cope without you first, so perhaps raising this at the offer stage is best.

If they aren't family friendly from the get-go, then do you really want to work there? If you are able to get one job offer, invariably you are able to get more. As ever, it's about confidence. You aren't asking for permission here, it's a fair exchange. You have identified how your skills are going to benefit their business and you are explaining what you want in return.

Confidence for mum and carer returners

Your focus is on selling the *value* you provide potential employers, rather than presenting your CV in gratitude. You should feel less vulnerable. The potential client or employer either appreciates that value, or they don't. However, taking time out invariably knocks peoples' confidence and if you are leaving a child at home then it can add to the conflicting emotions. Returning to work is tough. I've been in that situation myself, when for a while I felt I wasn't doing a good job at home or at work. Factor in expressing milk in the toilet at lunchtime and all the raging hormones. It's a tough time for mums. In many organisations, we have to have a strong shell and project a 'business as usual' exterior. While worrying about how we can walk out of the office at 5.30pm sharp to get to the nursery on time. I sympathise! Repeating the mantra of; *'If I knew I was at the top of my game here, how would I behave right now?'* can give you a reality check. And yes, another question is; *'If I was a man, how would I behave right now?'*

Many high-achieving women I coach are natural perfectionists, but becoming a working parent means we can no longer do everything perfectly. Now is the time when we no longer manage our workloads and balance home and family life to the standards we have set ourselves in the past. What do you need to do perfectly and when can things be good enough? There

3

will be plates you need to juggle; some you cherish and some you can drop altogether.

Navigating the boundaries between your personal and professional roles isn't easy. All the feedback and research shows stress occurs when work impacts on home life, rather than the other way round. Doing a sneaky online shop at lunchtime feels good. Taking calls when your kids are in the bath doesn't. Research by charity, *Working Families* in 2016 revealed that 29% of parents feel burned out often or all the time. In fact, 45% of mums start doing domestic chores as soon as they walk through the door, compared to 25% of dads. Mums are also the first port of call when childcare breaks down, by a factor of 2:1. It's hard to make work and family life balance. Get as much support as you can afford, to lessen the stress so you can focus on your priorities.

Now is a good time to revise your career goals and know why you are returning to work and what you are aiming at. Is this a time to reinvent yourself, to change old habits or patterns of thinking that could hold you back? You may feel anxious now, but once you have some experience back under your belt your confidence will return. Remember, confidence comes from action, not the other way round. Don't wait for it. Crack on and it will most likely catch you up. And if it doesn't; who cares, you are doing what you want, anyway.

When you go back to a job that doesn't challenge you and develop your skillset you will end up feeling frustrated and demoralised. You need a job where the challenges match your skills and as your skills develop you take on greater responsibilities. Otherwise, working parents or carers feel they aren't doing anything right, not being fully present at home and not succeeding at work.

I have seen many mum returners who apply for more junior positions, don't get shortlisted and assume this is because no one wants them now because of their career break. In fact, it's unusual for people to be hired in a job that is much lower in status than the one they had before their break because employers know that once their confidence returns they won't want to stick at it. If possible, go back in at the level you left. Certainly, at the level of your 'highest and best use' where you are differentiating your skillset and adding the most value you can.

As well as our own thinking holding us back, sometimes other people can also make assumptions about us that hinder our progress. For example, your manager might assume you are returning to work under duress, to pay the bills, and you are not motivated to take a promotion or you are tired from your caring responsibilities and unable to cope with too much pressure. They might be correct of course, or partially correct, but many parents think if they are going to work outside the home they might as well aim as high as they can. Don't let other people make assumptions about your ambitions or energy that can impact on your prospects. Make your ambitions clear and ask for the projects, support and opportunities you want.

3

It is important to re-establish trust with your colleagues and managers, particularly when you need some flexibility with your hours. Sometimes role responsibility can be ambiguous, especially under weak managers. What are the most important outputs of your job and how will you be measured? Make sure you deliver on the important stuff and that you are seen to do so.

Exercise: Balance your career and family life

Write down the answers to these questions in as much detail as you can.

- If you put your own selfish desires first, just for once, what would your career goals be?
- What's stopping you from aiming for these now?
- Are they really selfish or unachievable right now, or could you start working towards them?

3

This chapter is for women in particular, but is useful to everyone. It will help you make your voice heard; secure your seat at the table; and ask for what you want.

CHAPTER 18

Women: Man up

Cross the gender pay and promotion gap

A 2016 Women in the Workplace study by McKinsey & Co and Sheryl Sandberg's Leanin.org said that it will be more than a century before there is gender equality in the workplace. Their findings were that it has little to do with women opting out. Attrition is roughly equal between men and women, but women are facing barriers to advancement primarily due to gender bias. They face more pushback when negotiating; they get less access to senior leaders; and they receive less feedback. We have to push harder than men to be visible! That doesn't mean being pushy; it means pushing yourself forward and making people realise how good you are. You have rational opinions on the best way to achieve goals. They might not always be right, but they might not always be wrong either. Someone will agree with you and if other people are quiet, it doesn't mean they disagree with you: they may be considering what you have said.

Secure your seat at the table and make your voice heard

As well as 'leaning in' women have to 'speak up'. It is crucial to understand your value so you can make a valuable contribution.

3

Establish your personal brand and have the courage to speak up. Doing great work is vital, but it has to be noticeable. Be politically savvy: prioritise projects that make the greatest impact. Proactively provide your manager with a status update on your project and emphasise the achievements. What can you do the make your boss's life easier? Do it!

In August 2016 the Institute of Fiscal Studies (IFS) revealed that women earn 18% less than men on average. The gap balloons after women have children and the IFS raised the prospect that women are missing out on pay rises and promotion. It could be that women are more likely to work reduced hours of course, but that does not account for the disparity. Many mothers are now the breadwinners in their family so things are changing. There's a full chapter on negotiating your salary later, but I want to clear up some misconceptions I regularly hear from women I coach, based on my own observations and feedback from headhunters.

Don't be grateful

I have coached women many who are so grateful to be hired back into the workplace that they take a low salary 'to get a foot in the door'. They hope they will get an increase once they have proved themselves. This doesn't happen. They only get the annual increase and so are always on a lower grade than a more confident colleague who pushed for a higher starting salary. You are being hired because of the good job you will do and there is a fair market rate for your skillset. Companies don't say; 'Let's give them a chance'. They say; 'We have a problem and their skillset is the solution, what do we need to pay to get them on board?'

You know you are going to try your hardest to do a good job immediately. So why not push for the highest salary you can, that reflects that? No one remembers how much you are on. But they will remember your professional pride and confidence.

It's not pushy to negotiate; not if you do it professionally

Not only is it not pushy, it is expected of you. What's wrong with being pushy, anyway? Think of it as gamesmanship.

There are few jobs nowadays that don't involve some element of sales and employers expect you to demonstrate your skills in the way you manage your own appointment. It immediately marks you out as talent, one to watch.

'Although women think negotiating involves being aggressive and loud, good negotiation actually means not sacrificing what is essential to you, while allowing the other party to do the same: something that women are brilliantly suited for.'

On Becoming Fearless, Arianna Huffington

Put your hand up

As a general rule, women aren't visible enough to get picked for either internal or external promotion. Headhunters tell me time and time again they struggle to find women, not because there isn't an appetite now for mixed shortlists, but because women are less visible. We can make our own glass ceiling. It's not enough to be good at your job. You have to be visibly good at it too. Get out there, build your brand, be a 'go-to expert', speak at events, nurture your network and tell people what you are achieving. No fluff of course, pure facts. You don't have to be on the stage; have conversations with as many people as possible about what you can do and what you want to do next. Don't have lunch at your desk, when you can be building a relationship instead.

Believe in what you can do

The other common complaint is that women don't want to take the next step up, until they are practically already doing the job and feel confident they can do it well. I hate to talk in stereotypes, but men look at the 70% they can do, women look at the 10% they can't. A headhunter told me the executive men she moves usually want to take their team too, because they want good people around them who they trust to fill the gaps. Women move in a team less often, partly because we aren't so good at building these trusted networks (less rugby and other team sports, maybe) and also because we work more independently. Men share the pressures. Women shoulder them.

We reject promotion opportunities because we assume they might tip over our precarious work life balance. I find that male clients have that; *'I can do it until proved otherwise'* approach. They are rarely proved otherwise and the worse case is that they get promoted up the organisation when they do under another manager. I bet you have seen it happen?

Develop a laser sharp focus

Don't worry about the peripherals. If you can fulfil the main roles responsibility, you can do the job. Don't worry about 'everything else we might ask you to do' that's not important. I follow the Pareto Principle in focus and time management: 20% of your time goes on 80% of your output. Always, ensure your output is the main deliverable the company expects and understand which is your most important, sacred 20%. Don't sweat the small stuff. What Arianna Huffington calls sacrificing the important (someone else's important) on the altar of the urgent (on becoming fearless).

Don't always do the small stuff either

Stop automatically doing the low-level tasks or being the office mum. Keep your note-taking, tea-making, cake-making, tissue-offering and grammar-correcting skills to yourself.

Women default to doing jobs that make us liked. It is in our nature to want to please people. Sometimes, it can be politically useful to make a coffee, but if you want a leadership role, focus on your higher-level skills. I'm not saying you don't have to be an authentically nice person, but take yourself seriously as a role model for younger women at work too. Why should we put out the sandwiches at the meetings and clear the plates? There's nothing wrong with being helpful but; *'Sally is so lovely, we love having her around'* doesn't necessarily mean they are going to give Sally the highest pay rise when it is appraisal time. In fact, if budgets are tight and you are less likely to kick up a fuss, you are likely to be at the bottom of the queue. Be known for more than being nice and helpful. You are an adult woman now, not a nice little girl, programmed to please.

Get out there and known to the influencers

Develop a snappy; *'This is who I am and what I do'* pitch. Although, if you have caring responsibilities at home, it can be difficult to do out-of-hours networking. Don't worry about the events you can't go to. Force yourself to make more of an effort for the opportunities you get. You don't have to network, but find out about the people you meet by asking them questions. Remember it's not about you; it's about what you can do to solve their problems. You only find that out by asking questions. Never eat lunch at your desk, take 20 minutes to eat with someone else and cultivate new relationships.

Part of learning how to *Mind Flip* is asking; *'What would I do now if I was at the top of my game?'* Returning mums might also want to ask themselves; *'If I was a man, what would I do now?'* I hate gender stereotyping too, but you get my point.

For example, I was working with a fantastic American woman, who was earning around £140,000 and had decided to leave her employer. I asked her what salary she wanted next because I believe if you know exactly what you want and write it down, you are well on the way to getting it. She said; *'I think I am worth £170,000.'* I commented that generally speaking British women wouldn't have the confidence to ask for that level of increase. She said if she had been an American man, she'd

3

have lied and said she was already on £200,000 and wanted £250,000. I am not suggesting lying about salary, it goes without saying. But I love the chutzpah.

Another reason to get up the career ladder is that the higher-level jobs tend to give more flexibility and balance. More senior people have more choice in where they work and how they work because they have less supervision over the tasks they complete. The focus is on the output they get. What they do rather than how they do it.

Don't stay in a lower level job thinking it will give you less stress or more balance. Check your assumption. Often, the higher-level jobs have more autonomy, flexibility and balance.

Exercise: Personal brand check up

Write down the answers to these questions in as much detail as you can.
* What can you do to enhance your personal brand at work?
* How can you get more exposure for what you do well?
* Are you looking the part of the leader?
* Are you cultivating relationships with people who can influence your career?
* Make a list of people you need to have conversations with and do it.

3

This chapter has extra help for managing interviews if you are a disabled job seeker or have health challenges.

CHAPTER 19

Support for disabled candidates and people with health challenges

Health and disability questions

Employers should avoid asking you health or disability questions before a job offer has been made, including any questions about your sickness record. Once a position has been offered, they can make enquiries into your health, but only if they relate to your ability to carry out the role effectively. They can't say; *'How many days did you have off sick last year'* but they can ask if you have any specific requirements to perform the job effectively. They can ask if any adjustments need to be made to accommodate your needs. You are under no legal obligation to disclose your disability, but an employer cannot make reasonable adjustments if they do not know you have a disability. This can cause you problems in an employment tribunal.

3

There are many examples of people who don't get called in for interviews when they mention their disability on their CV. Of course, some organisations are more enlightened and more mindful of how hiring you will make them look good on tenders and bids for work. They are being compliant with the Equality Act 2010. You might want to mention your disability by including it in one of your competency-based answers. For example, how coping with it has increased your resilience, communication skills and time management skills etc.

This book wants to help you progress your career and my advice would be that if your disability isn't immediately obvious, wait until later in the interview process – or after the offer has been made – before you disclose it. The interview needs to be focused on how well you fulfill the role responsibility; not about your disability. Show them that you are by far the best of the shortlist first. All personal or health questions must also stick to your ability to perform the role responsibility. For example; they can't ask; *'How much do you weigh'* but can ask; *'Are you able to carry boxes that weigh up to 25 kilos?'*

You can't be asked whether you smoke or how much alcohol you consume either. There will be policies for conduct and substance use at work, but what you do in your own time should have no relevance to your suitability for the job. Of course, in the real world you need to fit in and looking healthy is expected of most professionals. If you have obvious health or personal issues bring these up as a positive. For example, if you are mid-way through a weight loss or gain programme and it is obvious you still have some work to do, then mention it as an example of your commitment, resilience, focus, wanting a new challenge and use it to score points.

How to manage when your disability isn't obvious
I have worked with clients who have 'invisible' disabilities such as brain injuries or who live with pain that isn't obvious to the rest of us. They have told me their lives would be easier if it was

clear to other people what they struggled with. So people could immediately make allowances for them in the way they would if they had a limb in a sling.

Remember, I'm not an employment lawyer; I'm here to help you get the work you want. But I know the work place is slightly less hostile than it used to be. The Equality Act 2010 has banned the use of pre-employment questionnaires, which force candidates to answer questions about their health, so there is some protection against discrimination. Larger organisations have workplace health programmes to support existing employees. However, let's be realistic. If they have a choice between two equal candidates, one with no health issues who will have a 100% attendance and productivity rate and a more vulnerable employee, who are they going to put on their payroll? And remember the young Masters of the Universe at the early stage of the filtering processes will have less sympathy than those of us who have seen more of life.

Mental ill health seems particularly embarrassing to deal with - people don't know what they can and can't ask you - no matter how well intentioned they might be. And there is still a stigma and bias about mental health issues. This is ironic, given that mental-health problems in young people is an epidemic of our social media age of cruel comparisons.

If you have a gap in your employment history because of chronic depression, or a bi-polar diagnosis for example, my reluctant advice would be to avoid telling them this if at all possible. Explain the gap in another way. Tell them what you did on your gap. Skate over why you took it.

Disclosing means you are protected by the Equality Act and discrimination against you can be unlawful. Back in the real world of course, discrimination is hard to prove. Unless it is an organization where direct experience of these issues can benefit you, then if at all possible I would keep it to yourself. I know one organization that prioritises hiring people with real life experience of these issues so they do exist, but they are a sad rarity. If you feel you need a more sympathetic environment, my suggestion would be to take a swerve from corporate life for a while - work in the third sector or public sector - where there might be more flexibility and understanding.

If you can't escape telling a potential employer and sometimes you have a duty to disclose information that could prevent you from doing your job, then make sure you tell them as much of what you can do, as what you can't. As always, you position your unique skillset so they can see what you can do for them first.

Curl your toes a bit and sell your brilliance first.

Here's an example of what one of my coaching clients put together to explain her brain injury.

'Since I had my stroke, funnily enough I have found that I am slightly more creative. I have weirdly become great at anagrams and crosswords, for example. I can still write great copy and if anything, have built closer client relationships both because of my experience and what I continue to do for them. The programmes I run have had greater uptake so it's all going better than expected and I know where my value lies.

However, the flip side of the enhanced creativity is that my processing skills are weaker. I am less strong at the detail of project management so I ask my administrator to do this. I put my energies into the strategic side, which is where they should always have been anyway. I also have a 'brain surgery done – got the tee-shirt' on my email signature so that covers me for any typos and I usually get someone to double check my copy before it goes out. I think people make allowances and they know I get results on the main things so it's not complete altruism. You know, I've had a tough time, but people want to work with me and in a funny way, it's made me stronger and more focused.'

The rules are the same for everyone. First, convince them of your unique value and skillset. And secondly, when they offer you the job, mention what you need to do your job well. Position it about best performance of the job, rather than a coping strategy for you, in an efficient, assumptive close.

'Just to let you know, I find that when I have substantial writing pieces to do, it helps to work remotely to get it done. Depending on workload, this could be a couple of times a week, but I have a great laptop with all the programmes we need on it. What version of the system do you use?'

You may wish to explain any health issues once you have a job offer, or when you join. Be business like and professional. Your disability is not your entire identity, only a part of it.

A client of mine told me how she revealed her health issues by explaining how managing the side effects could affect her work. As a consequence of her illness she got tired easily, so took regular breaks for fresh air to keep her energy up, then got back into the flow. She said in her last job people who didn't know her background had assumed she was a smoker. It was hard for her manager to object because she had subtly said that was the only visible sign of her illness and if they stopped her going out, they'd have to stop the smokers too. She was great at her job and well liked, so her coping strategies weren't a problem. The lovely twist to this true story is that people in her team started to go out with her and they all benefitted from the fresh air short breaks.

This chapter will help people who are more than 50 years old to know how to beat ageism, as well as plan for their retirement.

CHAPTER 20

50+; rip off the cardie

Ageism; real or perceived?

There is unquestionably some short-sighted ageism in selection processes. However, let's work with the assumption that employers want the best person for the job and some have the wisdom and experience to do exactly that. You don't care how old I am, do you? You want me to help you get better work more quickly. My age is relevant. I've heard it called being 'agenostic.' Recruiters are selling expertise and many of them wear their years of honing that expertise quite visibly. Sometimes 'perennials' in an office full of 'millennials' can be a source of stability and emotional intelligence, as well as ticking the box for a more diverse workforce.

I have listened to clients complain of perceived ageism, often with great justification. Many industries are notorious for having a shelf life for the over 50s; maybe even the over 40s. The Silicon Valley tech industry is notorious for their ageist culture. According to Lucy Kellaway in the Financial Times, the median age of employees at Facebook and LinkedIn is 29 and Google's is all of 30. She quoted Mark Zuckerberg saying; *'Young people are just smarter.'* Younger people might be cheaper; but they certainly aren't smarter. Who wants to work in firms that have

3

that blinkered mentality? It's a bit tragic to try and fit in with this kind of bigotry. At some stage these firms will wise up and realise that not only is this illegal; it is also foolish. It is the older people who have the money to buy their products and understand their customers and they need to employ them.

To be fair though, sometimes more mature workers can create their own problems. I've seen people give off a tired vibe of; *'We did it brilliantly in my old place and there's nothing you can teach me now, sonny.'* That's not the way to get work; we've established it's all about the target employer's ego, not yours. You have to play the game to a certain extent and show a desire to keep learning and a willingness to fit in. I'm not suggesting Botox and hoodies, just enthusiasm rather than the cynicism that can creeps up on us as we get older.

Of course, employers do make assumptions about older workers, even if they aren't actually discriminating against them. They can write them off for not having much energy left and presume they aren't as committed to their careers as they were. The reality can be quite the opposite. They are still productive even if they aren't reproductive any more. Post 50 can be a time when people devote themselves to their careers and become more ambitious, not less. They are in a sandwich generation of caring for both their children and their parents and the money is still important to them. They need to bank pension contributions because retirement dates slide further into the future, pay for carers for their parents or help their children come up with a deposit on their first homes.

This can also be a time when people want to broaden their horizons or revisit old goals. I have seen women who have built successful freelance or kitchen-table careers return to corporate life once they no longer have family responsibilities. They see this as their time now. Enlightened organisations, aware of their talent shortages, want the knowledge and networks these older workers can bring; it is their 'grey capital.' Leaving aside a few menopausal hormones (I can say that) more mature workers generally bring emotional maturity and wisdom to the team too and they make great mentors. In industries that tend to employ young bucks it can be reassuring for clients to see a few grey hairs; it adds credibility. Many people when they hit 50 finally seemed to get their act together, time has passed by and they don't want to waste a moment more. Being older brings clarity and focus on priorities.

I've seen people asking for flexible working to spend more time on outside interests (I see travel and triathlons come up frequently) and those caring responsibilities can creep into the week too. They might want to cut back on hours but still have the challenges and rewards that working provides.

Whatever your circumstances, your employer is often frightened to ask what you want unless you tell them. Push for those career conversations that managers are supposed to have with you, but often avoid. Organisations have great programmes now to support their young talent, women returners and diversity agendas, but the talent and retention of older workers is still overlooked. Surprising, when this is the talent in plain sight. Too much like an old sock perhaps; loved and taken for granted. More reason to be an advocate for your own career, by honing your brand identity and ensuring you state your current career plans and skills confidently. This applies to your current organisation, as well as on the external job market.

Tactics to get round perceived, or real ageism

Your CV and LinkedIn profile
Don't put in the dates of your education. That's the biggest give away. You don't have to detail all your job history either; you can summarise it under one heading of 'prior to 1990' for example. You can be really naughty and have a misleading date of birth in your email address. For example, Zenaeverett79 might suggest to people that was my birth year. On the subject of email

addresses, use a modern professional on; like gmail. You don't want to look like a luddite.

Make sure your personal statement is particularly punchy with a clear statement for where you are in your career now and the next challenge you want to tackle. If you are opting for reduced hours for example, frame the statement to explain why you are career orientated but want balance as well. Here is an example.

'Having worked in senior executive leadership roles for many years, I want to concentrate on my lifelong passion for complex forensic accounting, particularly within international financial services. I would prefer to relinquish people management responsibilities, allowing me to work a shorter week and pursue my extracurricular passions also.'

Remember to drop qualifications that date you, for example Pitman's Shorthand; especially if they aren't relevant to what you do now. 'O' levels are a definite no, as well these days. Only include the most up to date training courses, systems and processes to make you look current. Make sure you use a contemporary layout; a dreary old CV is a real sign of being old. Follow all the advice here. There is a list at the end of the book as a guideline with plenty more online. Don't layer your most recent job on top of your previous experience; nothing looks more dated. It goes without saying that it's not your years of work that count here. They show you have worked for a long time. Focus on the contribution you have made backed up by; of course, measureable achievements. You don't need to list everything you have done in a organisation. For example, you can say:

'Joined Proctor & Proctor as an Analyst in 1981 and worked my way up to Chief Scientist, a role I was promoted to in 2009.'

Show energy with great hobbies and interests that prove what a well-rounded interesting person you are, someone who is fun to be around. Include something sporting, if you can; even just saying; *'long weekend hikes'* is better than *'walking.'* Put something interesting in this section that they want to talk to you about. The interviewer wants you to be a positive force in the office, an example of what people can aspire to. Be a positive role model. Show that your brain hasn't flat-lined either, by including recent courses, qualifications and skills that you are developing. It shows you aren't stuck in the past and you can cope with change.

Your LinkedIn profile needs to be particularly punchy, to show you are up to date with modern office life and business networking. Demonstrate that energy with a great profile picture and don't make it out of date or blurry. Be bold and proud of who you are, don't pretend to be something you are not. As long as you solve their problems, they not worried about their expert's age. A few grey hairs add to the air of expertise.

At interview

Generally, I find more mature people are much better at stating what they want clearly. They don't have the patience to dance around. They have built up a solid body of evidence for what they do well, a laser focus on getting things done and life has taught them how to multi-task and manage their time ruthlessly. They shouldn't ask about your age of course and you never put it on your CV, but they can fish around by asking for the date you qualified. And of course, it's there for all to see on the passport you produce to prove you can legally work in the UK. They might ask you about your longer term career plans and that's when you hit them with your still burning ambitions. After all, it's not about how many birthdays you've had or how long you have been in the workforce. That doesn't mean you do a good job either; just that you have repeated the same actions many times. What is important is what you will do in the thirty

3

years of professional life most of us expect to have left: so tell them about your goals.

The danger comes when you feel resentful at being interviewed by someone younger than you. You don't answer fully and perhaps even point out where they are going wrong; errors on the job description, poor directions for example. If you feel nervous, you might do this also as a defence mechanism. You'll make your point but at high cost. If you are going for interview, prepare fully and show them you want to work there. You can always turn a job offer down if you feel you wouldn't be happy there, but give yourself the option and the interview practice. You also have to look like you fit in. I don't mean dressing like you are 20 years younger, but you have to overdress and look the business. Look like them on a very good day. You also need to look physically fit and healthy. Make the point that you have seen many developments/new strategies/leadership changes in your organisation/sector, so they know you are comfortable with change. Otherwise, less enlightened interviewers might assume you have sat at the same desk, with the same view and the same routine for decades.

Networking
If you've looked after people in your earlier career, now is the time to call in their favours. It is undoubtedly easier for all of us to get work through our network but this is especially the case when you are older. People hire people they know or people they know, know. Pick up the phone. Get out there; go to conferences and networking events on topics you are interested in, not just for the sake of it. There is nothing wrong with showing vulnerability by asking for introductions. The effort you put in to finding work shows them the effort you will put into that work when you start.

You may have built informal or formal mentoring relationships. Can you turn the tables and ask for help? What is it like working at X company? What are the challenges you are facing today at Y? Get their perspective on what's going on. Become a guru. Write a column, speak at events, give advice, publish on LinkedIn Pulse and join committees. Volunteering is good, if you've been out of work for a while, not least because it rebuilds your network and gives you new skills. You can include as the most recent job on your CV if that helps.

The most obvious plus for hiring older workers is that they are more likely to stay in a new role longer than their younger colleagues. This is a big advantage to HR who measure retention statistics and like stability. They might even feel it is a coup to get someone of your calibre, industry network, breadth of knowledge and industry contacts.

Plan for your retirement

Retirement, when it eventually comes is now seen as a transition from one career stage to another, rather than the abrupt change it used to be. Successful retirees plan for it by experimenting with new ways of spending their time before they stop permanent employment so the transition is less stressful. Modern retirement very often involves voluntary work and maybe paid part-time or portfolio roles. All of these should be planned well before time, by networking, establishing relationships and building your personal brand. A trustee role now, on the board of a charity, gives you governance experience that could lead to a paid non-executive role. It's worth keeping an eye on the future, thinking of different options and drafting your plans when the time gets closer. Selling your skillset with impact is as important now as it was in the early days if you are hoping to supplement your pension or passive income sources with some paid employment. Who needs a grey-haired guru like you to add wisdom, networks, credibility and expertise?

3

PART
4

FULFILL IT

This chapter shows you why you are more successful than you think.

CHAPTER 21

Reality check

The web is groaning with content about career success. Failure is now seen not just as okay, but to be welcomed as a necessary precursor to success; the 'no pain, no gain' philosophy that inextricably ties success with struggle - J K Rowling's *'rock bottom became the solid foundation upon which I rebuilt my life'* etc. The vast majority of us don't hit rock bottom and probably also won't reach J K Rowling's monumental levels of success. We can have a fair old crack at her success though; only a small percentage of her sales would do me!

Most careers actually bump along in that vast grey area in the middle; no great failures but our 'giant within' is never really awakened either. We get by, get the car, house, life we think we deserve and can talk about our work with a reasonable level of passion. But somehow, deep down, there is a feeling that; *'I could do better.'* And as we get older, that becomes; *'I should have done better'*.

Many people have this feeling that they have sort of failed, which may be the prompt for their job search. But actually most people haven't even managed to fail greatly enough so that the pendulum will swing the other way to great success. I call this

4

being an Average Failure (AF). 'Average' because most people, in fact, seem to feel this way, at least some of the time. And like most of our negative feelings, they come from an unhelpful and irrational way of looking at things.

Here are three thinking errors that make you feel less successful than you really are. It is, in fact about perception so now is the time to change the lens. As Derren Brown wrote in his great book *Happy* we are all trapped inside our own heads.

Thinking errors

1. You have set career goals that are too long-term and probably related to money.

I see a lot of people with this attitude. There's a long-term vision but this isn't broken down into short-term goals. *'I will keep going until the business is sold/I make Senior Partner/the kids are through university and can support themselves.'* The plates might be spinning, but you don't feel motivated, particularly in comparison to how you felt earlier in your career. You are bored, you've lost pride in what you do and have become the walking, commuting dead.

Don't wait for your life to change in a single huge leap at the end of the career rainbow. You need those big dreams; but break them down into steps along the way. Create immediate goals and deadlines that get your energy back.

What is the single biggest difference you can make now to achieve your ultimate goals? On that basis, where should you focus your attention and schedule your time? How will you measure your achievements, by when?

You don't always have to change jobs or do anything drastic; but keep the book for when you do. Change your focus and you will feel as if you are achieving again and are back in control. People who love their work are usually clear on what they do, why they do it and who benefits from their labour. They go to work to solve problems for other people (stakeholders, clients, a broader community) rather than financial rewards. These will come, but as a by-product of success rather than the only measure of it.

2. You think it's a bad thing to have stayed inside your comfort zone

You have no doubt been told that to be successful, you must challenge yourself, take risks and feel the fear. Tenacity doesn't appear often as a value in organisations these days, we are all a bit Bear Grylls instead.

Yet owning an area of expertise and making it comfortable is a real achievement. You've reached it through years of honest graft and refinement; your 10,000 + hours. I see greater performance from people who do a few things brilliantly and aren't frightened to stick with something to get it perfect.

There's nothing wrong with being comfortable and satisfied with what you do. In the old days, it was great craftsmanship. In a knowledge economy, it's your personal brand.

> *'An expert is a person who has made all the mistakes that can be made in a very narrow field.'*

> Niels Bohr, physicist and Nobel Prize winner

The only problem is if you get too cosy and scared to try something new. Use your knowledge and networks as a base to develop from, when the timing is right. Career transitions evolve in steps from that position of comfort, not massive leaps into the unknown.

4

3. You are working to someone else's definition of career success

The *'What do you do?'* question can provoke all sorts of reactions. Popular philosopher Alain de Botton says we are all 'job snobs' now. We judge other people by their job title, usually with some degree of comparison or envy. Our perception of careers comes from many sources: our parents; the people we went to school and college with; and our peer group, colleagues, neighbours and friends.

We benchmark our extrinsic success against other peoples; where we think we *'should'* be at by now. The anxiety this creates gets in the way of logical career decision-making. *'What will people say if I give up this cosy job to take a risk in a start-up? Everyone else gets into work at 8.00 am but I want to drop the kids off; will I be taken seriously? I could do this job remotely, but that's never been done before; should I suggest it?'*

How we spend our time should fit with our own values and priorities, no one else's. If you choose to work part-time so you can indulge your hobbies, that's fine. If you are the only mum who rarely does pick-up; that's fine too. Some people give up corporate life to work in the charity sector other people leave the charity sector to follow the money because they have aspirations that require higher salaries. These are your decisions and all of them are alright as long as they are your choice (and your nearest and dearest's choice too).

I've noticed how many of my clients make decisions as if they are being judged by some imaginary jury; perhaps by family, peers or colleagues. Do these people really have your best interests at heart and in any case how do they know what is right for you? How do you define career success versus a life well lived?

If your goals aren't aligned with your values, you won't achieve them whole-heartedly. If they are, then they can become even more ambitious. What's most important to you right now and does your diary reflect this: all most of us can control is what we do with our time.

I haven't yet met someone who really has it all, all the time; that elusive balance between career status, material goods, wealth, intellectual challenge, physical fitness, leisure, family and friends, etc. What is this 'all' anyway? It's another unhelpful pressure to feel you 'should' have a better work and life balance. You might think other people are more successful at juggling than you, but they are probably thinking the same about you.

The conclusion is, simply don't compare yourself to other people. It is hard to remove envy when we look at other people's lives. I've noticed that people aren't envious of people they consider to be out of their league, but feel more negative when people more or less at their level or where they 'should' be; over-achieve in areas that are important to them. They are not fussed about the CEO with her multi-million pound package, but resent the colleague who started at the same time but got promoted before they did. I've had to fake a joyous response when really lovely coaches in my network got their books published, while feeling genuine pride when other coaches get their doctorates. This envy can cloud decision-making. It's made me want to give up my publishing attempts, because I feel I can't compete. I had a client who had several job offers after redundancy and admitted he was drawn to taking the one that looked the best to his previous colleagues, rather than the one he felt most excited about.

My daughter has nailed the technique for unhelpful comparisons whenever I report back on another child's perceived achievements, usually learnt from their parent humble bragging in the playground. You know the type: *'I worry so much about Constance, she is studying so hard; it's impossible to drag her away from her books and she has no interest in parties.'*

4

Well, good for them, Mum.'

Alannah Atherton

Try it yourself. Benchmarking against your peers can be useful, but other people aren't you and as long as you: have goals; and are gradually moving towards them, then you are doing fine.

Now that you know you are more successful than you thought, what decisions should you make about your career?

Most people underestimate both what they have done in the past and what they are capable of doing next. It's good to know that we aren't alone in feeling like AFs, but it's such a shame that our perception gets in the way of pride in where we've got to. Unhelpful anxieties hinder achievement of our goals and become a self-fulfilling prophecy. Remove the doubts and think about raising the bar instead.

Intelligence is not a predictor of success

Here's a personal confession. I did a huge amount of bluffing some years ago to get myself on to my master's degree at Birkbeck. Although, I had secured a place to do my undergraduate degree more than twenty years before, I never took it up, so it was quite a feat to persuade the faculty that I could cope with the challenges of a post-graduate organizational psychology degree. Fortunately from my position of well-disguised ignorance, I had zero concept of those challenges and I wasn't in the least daunted by them. I soon woke up to them though; and spent many late nights sobbing over the statistics module.

One of the most fascinating parts of the course was learning how far exam success is a predictor of job performance and career success. Research by Richard K Wagner of Florida State University, quoted in *The Social Animal* by David Brook, surveyed the research results and found that IQ predicted only about 4% of variance in job performance and at best 20% to life success. IQ is a predictor of exam success, but there is very little correlation between IQ and life performance. Once a person crosses the IQ threshold of 120 there is little relationship between IQ and better performance. Phew!

The people who do best in life were proven by this research to have superior work ethics. They were the ones who had shown more ambition as children.

If you haven't read it already *The Social Animal* is a whole master's degree course all in one title. It would have saved me a lot of tears if I'd found it before.

Have you noticed how the cleverest people at school are not those who make it in life?
People who are conventionally clever get jobs on their qualifications (the past), not on their desire to succeed (the future). Very simply, they get overtaken by those who continually strive to be better than they are. As long as the goal is there, there is no limit to anyone's achievement.

'It's not how good you are, it's how good you want to be.'

Paul Arden, 2003

The upshot is that career success comes down to having strong goals and a work ethic to match. These factors are under your control.

4

This chapter will help if you suspect that things are not what they seem with your amazing new boss. Hopefully this will never happen to you, but I have coached enough people in this situation to want to include it in *Mind Flip*, so that if you are one of them, you realize you aren't alone.

CHAPTER 22

How to cope with a narcissistic boss

You joined an organisation to work for an amazingly charismatic, high achieving and powerful boss. They made you feel special, making great efforts to get you on board and sharing their ambitious vision for the future with you. You were flattered, even a little surprised and hoped some of their radiance would rub off on you.

Everything is fine in your probation period, but once you get your feet properly under the table, you have a hunch that something is going wrong; although you can't put your finger on exactly what. It is difficult to explain this feeling to anyone else without sounding paranoid.

- Your boss becomes moody and unpredictable and you don't know how they will respond to you. You don't want to upset them with bad news.

4

- You feel your boss is never satisfied with your work, that it's not quite good enough. You don't get feedback on what they want you to do differently.

- There are some occasions when you know your ideas are on the right track but only because your boss takes the credit for them. If you point this out, they turn on you, accusing you of being over-sensitive or not being a team player.

- Your boss fusses over the newest member of the team and at the same time starts to devalue the work you do, perhaps in public.

- Your boss blames other people for their own mistakes. They have extreme feelings about other people too – they are either flawless or written off as useless/evil/ enemies. People are either with them, or against them. Leavers who resign from their team are discarded, even disconnected with on LinkedIn. You feel guilty if you stay in touch with them.

- Your boss remembers situations and conversations in a different way to how they occurred, rewriting history. You start to question yourself, repeatedly thinking ;
'Is this me, or...?'

- Your boss starts to cold-shoulder you, cutting you out of projects and taking you off the list for meetings and emails. They deny it and roundly criticise your behaviour, even suggesting that you are a bully.

- Everyone else appears to idolise him or her. You fear you are going a little crazy.

If this sounds familiar, please realise - it is not you!

You are most likely working for a narcissistic boss. Narcissistic Personality Disorder (NPD) is more prevalent in males than females. Although NPD is thought to occur in less than one per cent of the general population, highly functioning narcissists appear to have leadership characteristics and it is not uncommon for them to crop up in senior and entrepreneurial roles. Most of them won't have a formal diagnosis, but a lack of self-awareness and empathy are hallmarks. Of course, many of us have some healthy narcissistic tendencies that enable us to push ourselves forward and survive corporate life. However, working for a true narcissist can put you in an extremely unpleasant, emotionally abusive relationship. If you have experienced this, you will know exactly what I mean.

Here's what you can do about it.

1. Do not take things personally. It won't be the first time things have played out this way with him/her. There will undoubtedly be other people who have had similar experiences to you, although they might not openly admit it. One of the consequences of this kind of relationship is that we often feel we are to blame; it triggers our own sense of shame, which can be lurking not too far from the surface. However, if you look closely enough you will realise that the narcissist doesn't really have close relationships; merely people that hang round, flattering them to achieve their own ends. The really strong ones move on sooner or later.

2. Keep up the pretence. Don't let them know you have seen through their mask of grandiosity and exaggerated talents. They rarely change; so you have to change your response to them. Narcissists have a strong vision of who they think they should be and are controlled by the shame of not living up to this ideal. Bursting their bubble is the worst thing you can do. Their response to any challenge will be aggressive and vengeful. Instead, let them live up to their

4

false view of themselves and even keep the image going by stroking their ego as much as you can bear. This is for your own self-preservation. Best of all, encourage them to move onwards and upwards. You might be surprised at the allies you have in this. How many times do we see this happen? People get promoted out of the way to become someone else's problem.

3. Take responsibility for your own behaviour. Co-dependents are people who allow themselves to be controlled or manipulated by other peope. They are natural magnets for Narcissists. Narcissists can't survive without people to feed their ego and co-dependents give up their own needs to fuel the needs of the narcissist; a perfect match. If you have a tendency to put other peoples' needs before your own and feel guilty when you stand up for yourself, then you are displaying the co-dependent behaviour that makes you the natural other half in the narcissist relationship. You may have had similar relationships elsewhere in your life. Get help to establish boundaries and drop your need for acceptance. The narcissist will quickly find someone else to idealise, devalue and ultimately discard: the classic three stages of a narcissistic relationship.

4. Get out of it. Even if you successfully use these tactics, working for a narcissist can lower your self-esteem and make you feel isolated, stressed and anxious. None of these emotions are good for you, your career or your other relationships. Carefully consider whether you want to continue working for this person, particularly if their behaviour appears to be escalating. If they remain a popular figure in the organisation – or one not to be crossed - your concerns might not be taken as seriously as they should be. Sending you off on sick leave with 'stress' solves nothing, but I see this happen often in these circumstances. You are not sick! Emotional abuse like this is damaging for people and

often taps into earlier patterns, becoming entrenched. Find professional support to get yourself in a healthy frame of mind so you can take back control, call a headhunter and move on.

It is far more likely that everything will go swimmingly in your new role. I would love to hear your coping strategies for working for a boss like this, in strict confidence of course. My contact details are at the end of the book.

4

This chapter will help you manage the challenges in the early days of your new role, as well as investigating the common factors of successful people and how to keep track of your success with regular career audits.

CHAPTER 23

Move forward

Congratulations! You've reached the other side and survived. You've found your new job or piece of freelance work or been promoted; signed the contract and celebrated. You've done a plan for your First 100 days, based on the questions that were asked at the interview, so you know where your focus should be and the expectations you have to meet. This is time to think about you; what you want; and how you want your work to work for you.

Be your own career coach and take yourself through these questions.

How will you know you have made the right decision?
- Project yourself forward six months.
- What will you be doing and how do you want to feel at work?

Do you need to reinvent yourself?
- There's a reason why you left your last job.
- Are there any habits you want to change or any new boundaries you want to put into place?

4

- If your role responsibilities are increasing how will you manage your time? Are you a perfectionist; is that one of the reasons you have done so well in the past?
- Do you need to start learning when being just good enough is absolutely fine?
- What beliefs and behaviours need to change in your new role, what helpful habits can you bring with you?

How will you manage your brand and skillset?

- What is the impact you want to make?
- Who do you need to influence?
- What do you want other people to be saying about you at work and what will they notice about you?
- If you are unsure you have all the skills you need to do your new job what are you going to do about it?
- Is this an opportunity to reinvent yourself as a leader?
- What new skills do you need to develop and what support do you need?

How will you manage your wellbeing?

- Start as you mean to go on with regards to working hours.
- Get used to the rhythm of the job.
- Can you have it all?
- How will you keep the plates spinning at home and at work, particularly if you are a parent or carer, returning after a break?
- How will you factor in time for you?
- Start as you mean to go on with regard to office hours. If you need to finish at six, then leave at six, don't apologise for it; just go.
- Learn the culture; whether you need to log on in the evenings and check messages, whether you can do calls to different time zones from home, if you are expected to respond to weekend emails when your boss clears their inbox and so on.

- Don't start something unless you intend to keep it up.
- Double check if your extraordinary contributions are strictly necessary to achieve your objectives.

Think about your time management and focus.

The Pareto Principle: Only 20% of your effort and time leads to 80% of your results. Do you know what that 20% is? And what will you do with the rest of your time? What are you doing that you won't be measured on and maybe can drop altogether?

And even further forward...

As well as landing the new job, my aim in this book is to help you build on your knowledge and confidence so you not only avoid future derailment but achieve what you are capable of.

I have been privileged to observe thousands of wonderful people in their careers and learn how they make decisions. Here are several of the patterns I have observed; in how they continue to build their brands and their profiles within their sector or their new job; as well as how they approach life in general.

Common factors of successful people

- To achieve your career goals you actually have to have decided on your goals! It might sound obvious, but many people never get round to this, drifting from role to role, rather than making decisions and feeling in control of what they do. And they might get to the top of a ladder they never wanted to climb. Rather than satisfaction, they feel disappointment. Perhaps a broader, horizontal perspective of work such as changing careers more and trying out different experiences would have given them more joy than the vertical path they assumed would be the right one because their peers or university cohort climbed it.

4

- Successful people listen more, do more, have a healthy perspective on failure and seek more advice. They nurture their networks. They put more energy into their careers and take action; lots of small steps towards achieving their goals. They combine a sense of what they want their working life to look like, with the energy to make it happen and they aren't frightened to try new things to see if they can do them.

- Confidence comes after action, not before. People who seem confident are simply getting on with things, regardless of how vulnerable they may feel inside.

- The more specific you are about what you do, the more likely you are to get hired and do well. The generic approach to job seeking ends in a dead end. Good candidates are very clear on what they do best and can articulate this.

- Our thinking and the lens through which we view our work can be our greatest impediment to fulfilling our natural potential. Our thoughts get in the way of what we are capable of. Poor managers don't help either.

- Selling ourselves doesn't come naturally, even to salespeople. We don't like talking about ourselves. The candidates who reach the top of the shortlist are able to get past this by focusing on what they have done in the past, not who they are. Past achievements and a clear reason for wanting the job, are the best indicators of future success in a role.

- Many of the most outwardly successful people are insecure about their careers. There can be a mismatch between what they do and their personal value system that makes their achievements seem hollow to them. This is particularly evident later in life once the financial requirements of work become less important. Earlier in their careers, they may be comparing themselves to other people who seem to be climbing up that greasy pole faster than they are, with all the trappings to prove it. In either case, it helps to remember that the person on the other side of the interview desk can feel exactly like you do. They might even be envious of you.

I am sure you are familiar with the advice to dig out your CV once a year and up date it. This doesn't mean you have to get it out there, but it keeps your focus on building your skillset. I hope you get some kind of feedback but often the more senior you get, the less you get formal or regular feedback. Unless there's a problem of course, but even then it can be delivered in a passive-aggressive way.

Just because you don't have a formal appraisal at work any more, there's nothing to stop you from doing your own. Every business has a strategic plan and a regular audit and it makes sense that you have one for our own career too.

How to do an annual career audit
Doing a regular career audit like this will help you feel in control of your working life; the good bits as well as what is lacking. You may decide to make big life changes, such as relocation, changing from permanent employment to freelance or moving to the third sector. Most people make smaller adjustments, such as requesting flexible working or making a conscious effort to work on projects that are more interesting and fulfilling.

Take stock of where you are now and where you want to get to, both long and short term. Enlist the help of people who know you well; friends, family and colleagues who may have a more objective vision of your skills and achievements than you do.

4

Make an appraisal of your career to find out what's important to you, where you want to be and if you're on track.

1. Start from the end and work backwards – your goal

Imagine your retirement party. Who do you want to be there and why? What do you want them to say about you? Are you on track to achieve this? It helps to work backwards from there. Write down your goal. Big, hairy, shiny, whatever you want to call it. Have a dream.

> *'Every great career needs one of these; no one stumbles into success without one.'*
>
> David Schwartz, 1959

Goals give you energy and it is your progress towards them, correcting your path when you stray off course that keeps you motivated. Having a clear great goal is like setting yourself off on automatic pilot; you'll find yourself making all the right decisions because you know what you are aiming at.

How will you feel if you get to the end of your career and you haven't done everything you wanted to? What if that book is never written, or that language never learnt? What will you regret not doing?

Once your formal career is completed, will you continue your professional interests in some way? If so, you may need to put steps in place now, such as developing products to give you an income, consultancies on the side, non-executive roles or trustee interests. Make sure you factor these in too.

Align your work with your values

As we get older we are less tolerant of situations that don't meet our needs. What do you value? What is most important to you? It could be autonomy, financial security, integrity, creativity, location, being an expert, sustainability, working in a team, working flexibly, gaining recognition, health, helping other people, learning, travelling, status and contributing to society. How does your work now match up to your values? What needs to change? In a perfect world, what would your working life look like and can you adjust your current way of working to achieve this?

Assess your achievements

What are you most proud of in the last year? What have you been thanked for? What's the brand you are developing; the reputation you have; and the particular achievements you are associated with?

This information will tell you where you should focus your attention in the future. And give you an excuse to celebrate too.

What didn't you do last year and why not? If you know what got in the way, you can do something about it. If you haven't achieved a goal it may not have been important enough to you; ditch it.

You may have had a tough time at work, but there will be silver linings too. For example, most people who have found a new job after redundancy say their lives have improved. List the positives to help you move forward.

Turn your goals into a plan

What do you want to have done when you look back on this year? Stick to no more than three goals, but make them substantial, exciting ones: aim for Pluto, worse case you'll hit Mars. Goals are simply dreams until you break them down into smaller goals and milestones. What gets measured gets done. Obviously tie these into the outputs and value you will be measured on at work. What support or learning do you need to achieve them?

4

Focus your time on what gets you to your goals

How will you spend your time more productively now you are clearer on your goals and values? Remember Pareto's Law; most of us get 80% of our happiness and desired outcomes from 20% of our time. How can you schedule your time to become more successful and ditch the time-wasters? Focus on the results that make the maximum impact. I love that Titanic analogy of spending your time looking for icebergs, not adjusting the deckchairs.

Every hour is important. Every task you perform is a step towards achieving your goal. My mother said to me; 'Yard by yard is hard, inch by inch is a cinch.' Results don't happen overnight; it is every small piece of action in the right direction that gets you to your end result.

After the appraisal

Set a diary date to do an interim career audit in six months' time, at least to polish up your LinkedIn profile and make sure your connections are up to date.

Nurture your network

Keep building genuine networks of people you want to help and who want to help you. Develop informal or informal mentoring relationships, both in your organization and externally. It can be an insurance policy to let people know that you are very satisfied with your current role, but you would consider an offer if it met some specific criteria.

*Doing regular career audits will ensure
that not only do you keep climbing the career ladder,
(whatever that means to you personally)
but also that your ladder is up against the right wall.*

Play it forward and become a mentor

You are now an expert at *Mind Flip*, clear on the value you provide and enjoying the spoils and satisfaction of doing meaningful work. Find a high potential person from outside your majority network and teach them the art you have learnt. Be a role model, introduce them to your connections and challenge their assumptions about their capabilities. Push them to set high goals and help them to maintain a laser focus on achieving them. It will be just as rewarding for you, as it will be for them.

I wish you the best of luck. Please keep in touch. If this book has been helpful to you, please go to my website and leave your comments and reviews. Thank you and feel free to contact me in any of the following ways. For a two minute animated version of the *Mind Flip* process, please visit:
https://youtu.be/VDpuj8IE1Ns

Email: zena@zenaeverett.com
Website: www.zenaeverett.com
Twitter: @ZenaEverett1

4

Zena's CV template

This is an example of a simple CV format. There many alternative templates available online. Decide which one represents you best and would appeal to your audience. Keep it to a standard font, such as Arial or Times New Roman and no smaller than an 11 font, but ideally 12. Any more than three pages and you might need to do some culling. Some people have a separate page at the back, listing published articles or technical qualifications. It's up to you, but everything you include on here think; *'Why am I telling them this?'*

Your name here

Email : (business like!)   Address:
Mobile:
No date of birth and no picture !

Your career statement here – *what you have been doing, what you want to do next, the skills you have to bridge between the two. What can you do for the reader? As succinct as possible and specific! Use key words that match the job description if you are applying to a specific advertisement or want to come up in searches for specific job titles. You will probably have to adjust this slightly for each application.*

Major achievements
You might want to draw the reader's eye to some substantial achievements that aren't obvious from the first couple of jobs on your CV. Eg:

Voted 'One to Watch' in the ADINC awards 2017
Number One Fashion Blog Daily Post
Top sales person, Computerpeeps 2017
Youngest person to scale Mount Kynance

Otherwise, skip this section and embed the achievements where they occur, so we can see which job they correlate with.

Career History
Job Title
www.employerwebsite.com
Company name, Location
Dates, month and year – most recent first

A few lines to summarise the key responsibilities/accountabilities of your role perhaps some indication of the size of the organisation or department to put it into context

- Bullet pointed key achievements. What did you do over and above your job description? What is your greatest legacy, what will you be remembered for? Each achievement should be just 3 or 4 lines long.

Repeat this for the full sequence of your working life. You may want to summarise 'with earlier career'.

Other Skills (for example)

Computing	Microsoft Sharepoint, Windows XP, Citrix Xen app, Deltek Timesheets
Methodologies	Agile, PRINCE2, ITIL v2, RAD, XP
Languages	Fluent French and German, working knowledge of Spanish

---

Education

(some people choose to put this before the career history)

Date	**University**
	Degree
	Perhaps anything relevant such as the subject of your dissertation
Date	**Secondary school**
	Eg: 3 A-levels, 3 AS-levels and 10 GCSE's (including Maths, English and Science)

Interests and Activities

Make these relevant to what you want to do if possible, particularly if you are changing careers. You might wish to include voluntary work here, or to put it into your career history – whatever is most relevant to the reader.

Referees

(you don't need to include this at all if you prefer not to, or need the space)

You might want to put: "Professional and personal references available upon request" – generally it is recommended not to give details of referees at this stage if you are posting your CV.

References and Research Sources

Paul Arden, *It's Not How Good You Are, It's How Good You Want to Be*, (2003), Phaidon

John Arnold, *Work Psychology*, 2005, Pearson Education

Alain de Botton, *The Pleasures and Sorrows of Work*, 2010, Penguin

Peter Brant, (26 February 2014) *Who's frightened of being Middle Class?* Social Mobility and Child Poverty Commission website, https://smcpcommission.blog.gov.uk/2014/02/26/whos-frightened-of-being-middle-class/

David Brooks, *The Social Animal*, 2011, Short Books

Derren Brown, (2016) *Happy: Why More or Less Everything is Absolutely Fine*, Bantam Press

Lundy Bancroft, (2003) *Why does he do that? Inside the Minds of Angry and Controlling Men*, Berkley Books

Nicholas Christakis & James Fowler, *Connected*, 2010, Harper Press

Peter F Drucker, *The Effective Executive*, 1967, Butterworth-Heinemann Ltd

Gia Campari, David Glassman, Michael Jeans, Patrick McHugh, David Peregrine-Jones, David Shannon, Benjamin Taylor: *The 99 Essential Business Questions to take you beyond the obvious management actions*, (2016), Filament Publishing Ltd

Arianna Huffington (2006), *On Becoming Fearless… In Love, Work, And Life*, Little, Brown and Company

Hough, LM and Furnham A. (2003). *'Use of personality variables in work settings'* in Borman, WC, Ilgen, DR, Klimoski, RJ and Weiner, IB (eds) Handbook of Psychology, pp. 131-69. Hoboken, NJ: John Wiley

Herminia Ibarra, *Working Identity*, 2003, Harvard Business Press

Herminia Ibarra, (1995), *Race, opportunity and diversity of social circles in managerial networks*, Academy of Management Journal, vol 18, pp. 673 – 703

Lucy Kellaway, Listen to Lucy podcast, 1 November, *Silicon Valley's corporate culture is ageist*

Kidd, J.M., (2004), Emotion in career contexts: Challenges for theory and research. *Journal of Vocational behaviour*, 64(3), 441-454

LeanIn.Org and McKinsey Women in the Workplace Study, 2016 https://womenintheworkplace.com

John Lees, (2016), *How to Get a Job You Love*, Maidenhead: McGraw-Hill Education

http://www.dailymail.co.uk/news/article-1370567/Middle-class-youngsters-barred-internships-Whitehall-police--white.html

Donal Ryan (2012), *The Spinning Heart*, Doubleday: Ireland

https://www.rec.uk.com/news-and-policy/research/recruitment-industry-trends2

David Schwartz, *The Magic of Thinking Big*, 1959, 1965 Prentice Hall, latest edition 2016 Vermillion

Daily Telegraph, 3 March 2014, *Working Class Children must learn to be middle class to get on in life, government advisor says.* Georgia Graham, Political Correspondent

http://www.telegraph.co.uk/education/10671048/Working-class-children-must-learn-to-be-middle-class-to-get-on-in-life-government-advisor-says.html

Anne-Renee Testa (2007), *The Bully in your Relationship*, McGraw-Hill

Tiederman, D.V., O'Hara R.P., & Brauch, R.W. (1963), *Career development; Choice and Adjustment.* Princeton, NJ: Princeton University Press

David Thomas (2012), *Narcissism - Behind the Mask*, Book Guild Publishing

Paul T Mason (1998), *Stop Walking on Eggshells*, New Harbinger Publications Inc

Alan Weiss, *Value-Based Fees*, 2002 Jossey-Bass/Pfeiffer

Lightning Source UK Ltd.
Milton Keynes UK
UKOW05f1528150617
303364UK00001B/110/P